MW01128936

"McKenzie Wark has done it again! With her personal journey into questioning the foundations of everything from how capitalism works to the way our bodies and very identities are under radical transformation, Wark breaks it all down. A must-read for those who are interested in the evolution of digital music and the way it has reshaped the world around us."

—Paul D. Miller, a.k.a. DJ Spooky, author of *Rhythm Science*

"With loving precision, McKenzie Wark's eyes and ears pay attention to the innumerable tiny interactions, gestures, and rites that make up the all-night drug-and-dance party. *Raving* radiantly understands the rave as a construction site for transitory kinship structures—a pocket in timespace that is a haven for fugitives from consensus banality—a miniature home world for the aliens already on this planet. Ravers occupy the city's abandoned places and turn them into zones of abandon, where identities dissolve, where you can lose yourself and find

yourself. Wark's work is a font of deliriously inventive and witty language—immerse yourself in her text to discover speaker demons, rave condoms, punishers, and sidechain time."
—Simon Reynolds, author of *Energy Flash: A Journey through Rave Music and Dance Culture*

Raving

Practices
A series edited by Margret Grebowicz

Fly-Fishing by Christopher Schaberg
Juggling by Stewart Lawrence Sinclair
Raving by McKenzie Wark
Running by Lindsey A. Freeman

Raving

McKenzie Wark

DUKE UNIVERSITY PRESS
Durham and London
2023

Printed in the United States of America on acid-free paper ∞

Designed by A. Mattson Gallagher

Project Editor: Liz Smith

Typeset in Untitled Serif and General Sans

by Copperline Book Services

Library of Congress Cataloging-in-Publication Data

Names: Wark, McKenzie, [date] author.

Title: Raving / McKenzie Wark.

Other titles: Practices.

Description: Durham : Duke University Press, 2023. | Series:

Practices | Includes bibliographical references.

Identifiers: LCCN 2022045869 (print)

LCCN 2022045870 (ebook)

ISBN 9781478016762 (hardcover)

ISBN 9781478019381 (paperback)

ISBN 9781478024040 (ebook)

Subjects: LCSH: Rave culture—New York (State)—New York. |

Gay culture—New York (State)—New York. | Subculture—New York

(State)—New York. | Techno music—Social aspects—New York

(State)—New York. | Electronic dance music—Social aspects—New

York (State)—New York. | BISAC: SOCIAL SCIENCE / LGBTQ Studies /

Transgender Studies

Classification: LCC HM646 .W34 2023 (print) | LCC HM646 (ebook) |

DDC 306/.109747—dc23/eng/20220922

LC record available at https://lccn.loc.gov/2022045869

LC ebook record available at https://lccn.loc.gov/2022045870

Cover text handwritten by Lira Yin.

"And thus, when knowledge has passed through infinity, grace returns; such that it appears in its purest form simultaneously either in that human physique which is none, or in the one that has an infinite consciousness—in the marionette, or in the God."

"Therefore," I said a bit confused, "we would have to eat from the tree of knowledge yet again, so as to relapse into a state of innocence?"

"Indeed," he answered; "this is the last chapter in the history of the world."

—Heinrich von Kleist, "On the Marionette Theater," trans. Luce deLire

For all my scouts and ravens

CONTENTS

ACKNOWLEDGMENTS

Practices series editor Margret Grebowicz asked me on July 27, 2021, if I could submit a book for the series by September 22, 2021. In a moment of pure mania, I said yes. Apart from commissioned articles I hadn't done any real book-project writing that I was happy with since I started hormones in 2018. Your request helped me break a curse, so thank you, Margret.

I already had some bits, at least. The opening paragraphs of "Rave as Practice" appeared in *Unter: Rave Posters*, vol. 1, *2015–2020* (Brooklyn, NY: Untermaid Products, 2021). An earlier version of "Xeno-euphoria" appeared in *Noon Journal*, no. 12 ("New Communities"). I also used a version of that text for Side A of a spoken-word Bandcamp album I made during the 2020 lockdown called *Lonesome Cowgirl*, over a mix by Nick Bazzano. It was also half of a talk I gave via Zoom for HKW in Berlin on Mark Fisher's "acid communism." The "Ketamine Femmunism" text grew out of the other half of that. Part of "Excessive Machine" was first performed with a track by Body

Techniques at *Writing on Raving*, a series initiated by Zoë Beery and Geoffrey Mak at Nowadays in January 2022. Thanks to everyone for the space to experiment with this writing.

Thanks for helpful feedback to the GiDEST seminar fellows at the New School and the graduate students at the Prague Academy of Fine Art. Special thanks to all my students at Eugene Lang College and in Liberal Studies at the New School.

Thanks to my Duke external readers, especially Reader Two, who had homework for me. Thanks to everyone at Duke. Thanks to Lira Yin for calligraphy.

Thanks to Trans Twitter. No, really. I've learned a lot from parasocial trans and trans-adjacent friends and acquaintances, some I know or at least have met IRL but many not.

Special thanks to early readers from the Discord and Signal rave groups, including Q, L, Z, and H.

I'm grateful beyond words to my New York queer and trans raver communities. A special shout-out to those who work in nightlife: on logistics, on the door, behind the bar, on sound and light, as safer space monitors. I see you, and I'm thankful for the situations you make for us, with their difficult poise between safety and possibility.

Cheers to everyone who came to my sixtieth-birthday ravelet at the (sadly missed) Bossa Nova Civic Club, and especially to Cedric, for your kindness to this old queen.

1   Rave as Practice

FIRST THING I LOOK FOR AT RAVES: who needs it, and among those who need it, who can handle their habit?

Sitting it out for a bit. In the yard, where it's cooler. These crip feet throbbing. I'm propped against—something, or someone. Delicious fatigue. Resting my feet. Drinking water. It's getting light. Contemplating whether to go home. Lost my crew—let's call them Z and E. Think they're still here, somewhere. It's all good. A moment alone, but not alone.

Looking over the crowd. In small groups, sitting, standing. I think I see B and H and maybe A. I like that it's mostly the crowd that needs it. I'm chemically predisposed to liking. Rolling on molly for a while now and am heading for the shoulder, where you roll off into the dirt.[1] Even in this irritating light these still seem like humans I want to be with. It's not always easy, being a middle-aged, clockable transsexual raver. Right now I'm in a situation where I'm neither shunned nor attracting attention.

This situation began when I first glimpsed the poster. Not an actual poster. My friend Q sent it by DM. A tiny square of visual information. I put the date in my calendar and cleared the following day. It's for a New York queer rave that's run since 2015. Its posters suggest a certain pocket world of possibility. It'll be a rave, sure. The DJs will be great. Maybe there's a bit of a theme. You won't know where it'll be but can probably guess.

The artwork intimates something else as well. Each poster takes over and repurposes some other style. Which is sort of the whole deal. Take over space. Take over machines. Take over chemistry. Play from inside the signs, the tech, the real estate. At least for a bit. There's no outside anymore, but maybe we can find some fractal world on the inside. Now that's a good rave.

On a good night, everything at a good rave comes together with just the right tension of invention and intention. Everyone has a part in it. Some of it is work: There's W at the bar, serving a mate soda. There's N shouldering a monitor. There's S the promoter on his hustle, handing out drink tickets. Here's O with a big hug and a warm smile. But it's no fun for anyone if you just come to consume their labor.

Most of the New York queer and trans rave crowd gets this. Some come to serve looks; some come to leave their sweat on the dance floor. I'm the latter kind. I want to be animate and animated on the floor. A node in a rippling field of fleshy instances that tipple around the pulsing air.

That's what a good rave promises: Take in this situation. Add to it. Vary it. Update it, freshen it. Add an accent, a move, in time. The moment will pass on to the next no matter what you do. The rhythm machines exceed us. They're relentless.

They've displaced what was once called history. There's space between the beats, though, still to be.

Those beats are calling. I need to be back on the floor. I rested these crip feet enough to go back for more. I weave back through the topple of bodies splayed out in the yard. Back through the threshold. Where it's dark, hot, loud, a fog infused with trinket light. The beats invoke me. To this time inside the machine that we're all in, that goes on regardless, but within which here, in this lovingly crafted situation, art of many hands, we shall burn with animal fury, until it stops.

Dancing up close to DJ Goth Jafar. This girl next to me— let's call her F. I don't know what we are. Friends with benefits, maybe? Or maybe we're just occasional rave crew now. Anyway, tonight—she's on it. And it don't just mean a whole cap and stem. Pure motion, pure delight. She needs it. Sweat sheened. I go into rave mom mode. Not that she can't take care of herself. She saw combat, in a former life, in another gender. Touch her lightly on the shoulder. When she looks over, I mime and shout, "Water?" Check. I fetch.

Next to her is what my rave friend B calls a *punisher*, although as we shall see not the worst kind. He is someone who is going to make it hard to get your rave on, one way or another. He stands stock still in front of the DJ, checking his phone. Then he turns to his friend, another punisher. They have a loud conversation. Then he lifts up his beer can and sprays the contents on those around him. When I return with water, F has moved away from him.

Raves serve a lot of needs, interests, desires. For distraction, entertainment, exercise, dating, cruising, and so on. Those might be met by other practices just as well. I'm interested in a specific set of needs and a particular range of people for whom the rave itself is the need.

Not interested in punishers. Even less in what H, another rave friend, calls *coworkers*: people who just want a night out so they can talk about it around the office on Monday. Having avoided the punishers, now we're stuck next to a coworker. He's into it, but a little too hard. Not that I'm judging; I know the feeling. But it makes it impossible to be dancing next to him. Hyperfast, erratic movements, throwing himself around, like he's the only one here. We move again.

I'm interested in people for whom raving is a collaborative practice that makes it possible to endure this life. There's a lot of metaphors I could throw at this: rave as addiction, ritual, performance, catharsis, sublimity, grace, resistance.[2] Let's not assume too much about it before we get there. Let's have some *concepts* of raving emerge out of some participation and observation.[3] I'm going to take you raving.

My practice for writing about raving will be to describe some situations, in some messy, heterogenous detail, highlight some emerging concepts, and then wrap it all up with a distillation of those concepts before the beat stops, or rather, before the book ends.[4]

Call the first layer of writing style here autofiction, if you like.[5] I'm in the writing. Hi! This is me. The stories here are fictions dancing around the facts. These things did not happen. The person to whom they did not happen is me.

Call the second layer autotheory, if you like.[6] It's writing that needs to gather concepts from situations more than it needs to extract stories from them. These situations being raves.

What is a rave like? A jackhammer in a sauna. To rave, to rove, to *rêve* (dream).[7] If it's called a rave, there's some expectations: It will go for a long time. That might need a little chemical assistance. There might be some socializing, some flirting, even some rave sex, but we're here to dance—to the point of exhaustion.

There's different kinds of raves. We'll be going to queer and trans-friendly raves in Brooklyn, New York. There's a few legal venues that the ravers I know favor, not always queer or trans, but where, depending on the night, we might be a flavor. Mostly, we will be in various venues of varying degrees of illegality, the location released only on the day.

The music will mostly be techno. Repetitive, four-to-the-floor beats, from about 120 to 140 per minute. Few if any vocals. Few sounds that bear any relation to any recognizable musical instrument. Some say techno came from Germany, but to me it's Black music. Which for a white girl like me comes as a gift, and one many of us use to other than original purposes. Within techno's surround of sounds and beats, there's been sonic situations for all kinds of temporary life, that of queer and trans people among them.[8]

DeForrest Brown Jr.: "Techno, as a historical artifact, derives its central premise from the act of African Americans dreaming of a future beyond the structural failings of a post-industrial collapse in the late twentieth century. Formulated out of a conceivably intuitive response to the urban degradation plaguing Detroit and other cities around the United States in the early 1980s, techno—rather than a generic component of a globalized music technology cartel and drug-induced nightlife economy—is evidence of post–civil rights era Black youth adapting to their exposure to consumer technologies in the industrialized Northern states. Detroit techno—a concept of sonic world-building and coded information exchange born out of a centuries-long lineage of African American struggle and insurrection—would eventually be exported, repackaged, and financialized within foreign markets to be assimilated into the British and European post-colonial drug and rave revolution—replicating the profit-oriented process of extraction."[9]

The irony being that the situations created by those of us from the global queer drug rave world are also now sites of extraction.

In contemporary Brooklyn raves, we will often be in the company of other trans people, like me mostly white, although mostly much younger. Trans people are a small but curious subset of ravers, and I have theories as to why. We'll come to that. At the rave, different kinds of ravers meet, and we'll meet some of the other kinds. The point of view will be that of this middle-aged, middle-class, white transsexual dance freak.

It's not my first rodeo. I came back to raving as a practice after a twenty-year chillout. There will be hazy memories of eighties and nineties raves, but I'm not interested in "back in the day." This is a story about finding something elusive in the nowadays. Something I came back to and am learning with a certain naïveté—an openness to folly, to findings that come from getting lost.

I did get lost once. Mixing molly and ketamine and weed like an overeager coworker. Am at it hard; everything aches. Can't find the exit to this sweet warren of a venue. Making a firm decision not to panic. Maunder the multiple rooms, the yard, sampling moments, situations, until the doors open and we all tip out. Daylight prisms through sweat.

I can handle myself at raves. On an overlit floor, into a dazzling madison moore set, loving where they're taking my body. Strobes flash. On way too much psilocybin. Finding it hard to balance. Everything's squirming. Stop, sip water. Sidle around the edge of the dance floor, touching the wall. I don't see any of my crew of the night, but there's A and U. "How's your journey?" A brief chat, already grounding, then moving on.

There's a sofa two stories up metal stairs, next to the darkroom where the circuit gays fuck. Head for it. Nobody here. Lie down, do breathing exercises, come back to some fuzzy but habitable embodiment. Check I have my silver rave bag. Drink more water. Go check in with Z, with whom I took the shrooms, to see how her journey's going.

Drugs are a part of rave culture, but sober raving is also a thing. I take a break in the midmorning to go home and nap. Come back clean for the closing set. The room, a miasma of fog and sweat. Kip Davis, the lighting designer, bouncing colored strobes off the vaporous air itself, refractions zagging. A hand reaches out, and I see it's attached to R, looming over the gloam in her six-inch pleasers. I'd intended to hang back but turns out I need it: to slip and shimmy myself to the front of the room, lose all awareness of brain and body, and trip hard just on the situation.

It's tempting to romanticize such moments. Mostly it's just a grind, the body granulated into sound, light; selves loosening into others. It might take hours. The ravers I choose to be around, those who need it and can maintain, are patient. It isn't grace, but not unlike grace, it comes when it chooses, not when you want. I don't know why I need this, but I need it. Others do too, maybe it hits the same way for them, maybe not.

Trans people are not the only ones who dissociate—but we tend to be good at it.[10] We're a kind of people who need to not be in body or world. The body feels wrong. The world treats us as wrong. Dissociation can be debilitating. And also sometimes not. I used to write a lot, in dissociated states. Then I transitioned, and couldn't write at all. And yet still needed to dissociate. I felt better about being embodied, but the world didn't. So—raves. And out of raves, the writing came back, slowly.

I want to recover at least some kinds of dissociation from the language of psychiatrists. I want to find ways this disability can also be enabling.[11] A way to find out things about the world. So now I have two dissociated practices that I need to live: raving and writing. Raving got the writing going again. It's a challenge to bring them together. It's taking patience, and practice.

I mostly write theory, so it's tempting to start with theory. I can resist anything except temptation—but am tempted by nothing so much as an exception. Let me break out of the autofictional groove with a quick dip into theory texts, to acknowledge some gifts. Firstly, the concept—both more and less than a concept—of the *surround*. That under and around, that refuge, hacked out of thickening air, this other city, underlit, undergoverned.

Harney and Moten: "Having looked for politics in order to avoid it, we move next to each other, so we can be beside ourselves, because we like the nightlife which ain't no good life. We ask and we tell and we cast the spell that we are under, which tells us what to do and how we shall be moved, here, where we dance the war of apposition. We're in a trance that's under and around us."[12]

Back in the summer of 2020, when a chunk of Brooklyn refused to acknowledge a police curfew and was on the streets for Black life, as Black life, a friend described it as a "Black rave." The rave, techno, nightlife, surround: they're all, among other things, gifts of blackness.

Harney and Moten: "But blackness still has work to do: to discover the re-routing encoded in the work of art: in the anachoreographic reset of a shoulder, in the quiet extremities that animate a range of social chromaticisms and especially, in the mutations that drive mute, labored, musicked speech. In those mutations that are always also a regendering or trans-gendering lies blackness, lies the black thing that cuts the regulative, governant force of (the) understanding."[13]

That the rave is one of several gifts of blackness, that's the first (and last) thing to say about it. A gift that already gestures toward transsexuality, even if it doesn't always feel (like) it.[14]

The second theory bit I want to borrow from is a different history of practices. Drawing on the writings of the situationists, let's think of a rave as a *constructed situation*.[15] A situation is where agency meets concrete forms that shape its expression. A constructed situation brings a certain intention to how agency can express its willfulness, its need.

The rave situation is a temporary, artificial environment made by the combined labors of the promoter, DJs, lighting designers, sound engineers, hosts, and all those paid to make it happen. They construct a situation that confronts the ravers with a set of constraints and possibilities. The ravers bring their freedom: their moves, raw need, and their arts of copresence.

For the situationists, the constructed situation had a revolutionary potential, for what the form of life could be after the abolition of the commodity, the spectacle, the whole oppressive totality. I remember some of those intentions still being present in some eighties and nineties rave scenes.[16] Today's raves are hardly a situation that prefigures utopia. They cannot prefigure futures when there may not be any. The constructed situation of the rave may be all some of us have—even if the revolution comes.

Morgan M. Page: "I've never been under the illusion that my kind will survive the revolution."[17]

Situation and story, two contrapuntal elements of prose writing.[18] This text is mostly situations, but if you want a narrative, here's a grand one: History and capitalism were dating. History was seeing other people, so capitalism really tried to look like the best of all possible worlds. Then they got married, and capitalism stopped trying so hard. And then history said, "Remember my vow, 'til death do us part? Well, do you think I was kidding, or not?"

Xeno-euphoria

I AM ONE OF THREE TRANSSEXUALS, stepping from the Lyft, somewhere in Brooklyn. Q steps out first. She looks incandescent, Instagramable under streetlamps and the warm glow of brake light. But then maybe it's me who's well lit.

I canter after her while Z brings up the rear. Those two are young and pretty and hot in raver black, while I'm in my white Rick Owens viscose dress, magenta platform Converse, and a strappy little leather bag by Hayden Harnett, in silver. I look stylish, but still feel more confident we'll get in if I'm sandwiched between these two far more fabulous t-girls.

Q sashays straight past the waiting line with a slender finger in the air and announces, politely and with a confidence I now know she doesn't always feel, that we are "on the list." Door bitch, cool yet respectful, clocks us. Holds us back for a moment. An eager crowd forms up behind us. "How many are you?" she asks. "Three." She ushers just the three of us through the door into the embrace of the sound and the threshold closes behind us.[1]

It's not widely advertised, and sometimes honored in the breach, but at this rave, trans women can enter for free. Or rather, the dolls are free.[2] All dolls are trans women, but not all trans women are dolls. I'm not. Neither are Q and Z, although tonight they might look like dolls, short of a close read. The dolls are more high-femme, might do sex work, are more likely attracted to men. They have nowhere but the night. The dolls also have their own scenes. Not my stories to tell.

That the dolls enter free is an ambiguous policy. It's meant to attract the pretty ones. A few spectacular transsexuals who know how to handle themselves and can dance all night give the proceedings a luster that no amount of queer cis women or gay cis men can quite muster. Although at the end of the night the coworkers will think all of us exist only to amuse them and make them feel like they just walked—on the wild side. Doot da doot.[3]

Later, when I talk to DJ Nick Bazzano about it, he has a different take. "You have to water your friends" he says. "The rave is like a mirror, a mirror ball, of the precarity of queer existence. It's about who knows how to improvise, who will trust in improvisation as an immanent form of social practice. So that's who's on the list: people who can't afford tickets, people for whom it's not a commodity experience, people who make it happen. You could call it *reparative discrimination*."[4]

It was Q who led me back, through the threshold, into the *rave continuum*, where every rave seems to join and fold into every other. It was she who got me dancing again.

We met on Trans Twitter, then IRL at my regular coffeeshop. Somewhere in that long conversation, I mentioned to Q how, before transition, dancing was one of the few times this body felt at home. Particularly if the music was techno. My theory being that it's a music, or more like a sonic technology, made for aliens. Being made for aliens, it's a sound in which no human body is more welcome than any other. Being no less at home in it than any other body, I feel like this body belongs, in techno, when I dance. "Well one of the better New York queer raves is this weekend," she told me. "We shall go together."

My presence at the rave didn't go unnoticed. Among the people who clocked me was Nick. It turns out that when not throwing raves in the underused industrial *junkspace* of Brooklyn, he is writing a dissertation about it.[5] Nick and I arranged to meet over coffee, in daylight hours.

"You walk into a situation that has gay rules," Nick says. "You can be fabulous if you want, but it doesn't have to be about that. Your style can be practical or tactical. Bring a nonentitled attitude—and a fan. It is all about who is coming to co-create the space, who you can gather so it will self-organize."

It's not queer utopia.[6] Even on a good night, there's punishers and coworkers. Encounters, good and bad. Some moments in the rave continuum: I am at the bar getting mates before Juliana Huxtable starts her set when dude comes up and shouts straight through me, as if I'm not there, at his dude on the other side of me, squabbling about what drinks to order. I feel the sweat breeding off him, he is that close. When I call him on it, he tells me to "relax."

The beat crossfades to another, elsewhere in the continuum. Their smile is beatific. They are rolling hard. They came with F, who then went off elsewhere. As is her style. They keep asking me to help find her, but on instinct I just give them water and send them off in the wrong direction. They don't find F, they find me, on the dance floor. Dancing close, proximity alert. They keep knocking into me. Being big, strong, and tall to my spindly limbed slightness, they send me flying, then catch me, all smiles. I slip off through the fog. Later I find out they'd sexually assaulted F before they even made it to the rave. She still took them home and railed them. Hard.

I feel fingers tickle my nipples. Proximity red alert. Only to find some twink is playing air synth along to the mix, eyes closed. He apologizes sweetly. I smile back and reposition. Now I'm playing a dancing Goldilocks to three bears, each in matching webbed harness around their broad and sculpted torsos, with a little LED sign at the solar plexus that says CUNT. The musky smell of man sweat so strangely appealing I question my lesbianism. Did they share their poppers with me, or was that someone else?

To be free of a world that hates us, disrespects us, misunderstands us: it's almost impossible, even in New York City. A good rave, on a good night—that is where I can feel like my body is not an anomaly, or rather: not the *only* anomaly. It's a distribution of anomalies without a norm, anomalous only to each other.[7] That's what a good rave makes possible. Although let's never forget that we took this configuration of fugitive possibilities—from Black people.

It's better than the world outside. Rewind back to that first night, the night of my reentry into rave culture after a twenty-year absence, Q and Z and I stand on a Brooklyn street, waiting for a car service to come pick us up and take us to it. Z tracks the car on her phone as it approaches. We watch it arrive. The driver slows, clocks the three transsexuals waiting for him—and speeds away. One star.

Such insults are unpleasant but minor compared to what many other queer or trans people, particularly if they aren't white, endure every day, everywhere. But I want to write not about trans pain but glory.

There's kinds of nightlife situations that're constructed to be exceptions. For some it's the only place that feels even relatively safe. And for some these mostly white queer raves are not even going to consistently provide that. But on a good night, there's the possibility that some few people for some few moments—might get free.

Taking a break with friends in the yard, I say, in all innocence, probably to A or O, that this is a better rave than many I'd been to in the nineties. I'd had a pretty good guide to the Berlin scene at the time. The wall had just come down. As if by geopolitical magic, a whole chunk of city suddenly appeared in the bourgeois world, and its burghers wet their lips at all that property. But nobody knew who owned it. In the gap between magic and property, the raver mice came out to play.[8]

I remember following my Berlin techno piper through the byways of the darkened city, to a highway, and onto the median strip in the middle between the lanes. Down a concrete service stairwell to a metal door. A bang on the door. It opens a slice, fogged light and muffled beats issue. An exchange of phrases and glances. We're in. To what seems like the toilets of an abandoned subway station. Small, dark spaces, laced with beats and bodies. Hard beats, unadorned, square waveforms.

A flat yellow pill, three bottles of water, and some TARDIS of time later: back up the stairs, into the hard read of sunlight. Wandering about, happy, hungry, and tired.

I remember being taken to another Berlin spot. Those weird East Berlin streetlights. Broken pavement. Nondescript building, brick and barred windows. Dumpster and graffiti. Box of a room with a bar, some stools. Down precipitous stairs to a basement. Smell of dust and rust. Metal slots in the wall. Another flat yellow pill. Men in combat boots and camo, strangely chill. Later I'll figure out that place was Tresor.

I remember going with Edward, my boyfriend, back when I was attempting to be a gay man, to some nineties Sydney rave. Those ones were also usually in some urban junkspace nobody has quite figured out how to flip. I'm daring to wear a skirt and padded bra, fluoro yellow. Edward doesn't love these femme effusions, but he is humoring me. We line up in the cold outside a seemingly empty warehouse. Then we're inside, and it's a sculpture, curving plywood surfaces and dangling mobiles.[9]

DOOF DOOF DOOF DOOF. Our pills pop. I'm on my back on the plywood platform, drawing him down onto me, into me, sweat breeding from flesh. Lean head back over the edge, see upside-down people watching us. Close my eyes. Open them twenty years later. Cross-fade to now. That memory track beat-matched to this in the *rave continuum*. The topology of flesh-time folds to seamlessly cut that beat to that, to this.

Harron Walker: "The three girls lost track of each other as Cassie and Melanie left the dance floor to pee and Natasha went off to wander on her own. She found herself in the dark-room where all the circuit daddies and techno twinks went to fuck. She was neither of those things, nor had she ever been, but there was something about the sensory-deprived orgy that drew her in. There was a complexity she found lacking in her now thoroughly heterosexual sex life, as well as a simplicity: All these men needed were their assholes, poppers, cocks, and lube, and a world of possibilities opened up before them. Just then, Natasha felt a hand on her breast."[10]

And now, another now in the rave continuum, it's somewhere in Brooklyn. Techno with a retro acid flavor, but I'm wearing black: sequined top and miniskirt with the same magenta platform Converse. I'm in the bar area just with Q, as Z and E went home together already. We're drinking mate sodas, the liquid glowing orange in this light. Her face pointillist with sweat, beading through a canvas of makeup.

"Where did you get those shoes?" she asks.

"They're vintage, honey, same as me."

Eight beats pass.

"I'm sorry I've been a bit distant," she says. "I just don't want to talk about trans shit. I'll never disown who I am, who we are, but I don't want to be defined by it."

"Me neither," I reply, through the noise. "I've reached the point where it's just part of my life, not the whole of it. But sometimes I just need to be places where it's not too much of a thing."

She smiles: "More dancing!"

I follow Q, minnowing through the crowd. I've not yet relearned how to be nimble at weaving through the branching limbs. Apologetic gestures. She heads for the front of the stage, a space I've not been in a long time. The crowd is a dense thicket two meters out but when I crash through that tentacled mass there's a little clearing up front. I see her, right in front of the DJ. She's found K, gorgeous in the aquatic dark, as stray beams silver off her black vinyl jumpsuit. I'll learn later that K likes to spend the whole night there. A habit I'll soon acquire. Hugs and smiles, and back to dancing.

"What would a class analysis of a rave look like? Bad, probably. Maybe it's about class destiny rather than origins. What class does it create? Are ravers an immanent class?" Nick let the questions hang in the air. Daylight delirium. It's mental. It's in the night that we go with our bodies to find out. As much as I love a good concept, theory's the (not-quite) opposite of rave as practice.

DJ Volvox is close enough to touch. There's an empty bit of this pullulating space-time at stage left. Edging into it, the bass blasts so hard it hurts. I fish earplugs out of my silver bag. A delicate operation. If dropped—gone. With a little tech prosthesis, a body can be happy, in itself, in a situation. Earplugs in, and I'm entangled into this bass-strung warp of the weft at stage left.

The alien clamor of computation patterns a chronic 140-BPM situation. The dense, hot, wet, beat-stricken air, teaming and teeming with noise, sticks like meniscus, passing perturbations through skin as if skin's not there. It's all movement, limbs and heads and tech and light and air bobbing in an analog wave streaming off the glint of digital particles. Getting free.

Porpertine Heartscape: "Underground party for magical girls. The strobe light is a magical girl, spamming transformations at hyper-speed, frothing out of her mind on a superdose of girlchunks cut with biomech piss crystals. Isidol doesn't know how much time has passed, or if she even went to the restroom yet, she's gone so many times tonight, traveling to that sterile filthy room in spasming time-leaps through the crowd, the background tension of knowing the euphoria is ticking down, which is scary because life has no meaning for them, and only this xeno-euphoria they pierce into themselves feels worth existing for, the alien visitation that comes and goes but is not naturally produced by the body."[11]

The state of *xeno-euphoria*: Time becomes stringently horizontal. Neither rising nor falling, just sideways swelling and slimming. The body slots in, to time, finding itself stranded through itself, through losing the form of its being in time. I have to be patient, open, present for it. Let thinking flake off and fall away from the I. Then comes the pretty strangeness, into this body, out of the drugs it took, the beats it endures.

This is the need: that for a few beats, or thousands, I'm not. Not here. Not anywhere. In the place where there's usually me, with all her anxieties and racing-racing thoughts and second-second guesses, there's just happy flesh, pumping and swaying, tethered only by gravity. A trans body homing in on its own estrangement, losing itself, in these alien beats, among this xeno-flesh. Trans—the crossing—toward—the stranger's gift—xeno. This body that doesn't dance very well but loves to be gone anyway in the sway. Or so I imagine. I'm not there to notice. It's what I feel, or rather felt, happen. After it's gone.

Then that becomes something else. Without me knowing it, thought splinters, shards out sideways, north, south, east, and west, free jazz solos flocking around each other. Body and mind, both home, both happy, both into each other, both free to see other people, to be polyamorous with time. Welcome to *ravespace*.

Jessica Dunn Rovinelli: "Ravespace is dissociation, pure id and pure superego and nothing else. It can provide space for existing within and without the body simultaneously, a state of freedom that requires endless re-extension. Hence the possibility of addiction, physical or mental, the queer/trans sense of wellness, and the endless proliferation of new forms of movement alongside endless proliferation of stasis."[12]

Murmuration of thought, flocking and flying, whistling by as this body splashes into the squelching acid sonic goo that Volvox resurrects from the deck. The acid Nick was talking about: "Acid sound is analog. You twist the knob like you twist a nipple. The sounds all come out of fucking with machines. You use the sounds of capitalism to destroy the economy of taste. It's queer sonic materialism. It's a disruptive topological function that will fold you out when you can't get somewhere else. Acid is a technology of the non-self, an aesthetic performative function. It plays on the experience of the topology of totality. One that allows for you to see that the topology of totality is mutable."

This situation, modulating between dissociating into enfleshed euphoric oddness and ravespace polyrhythm, lasts as long as it lasts. The self always surfaces again, and probably just as well. Sometimes the I comes back online in flesh just to read the dials. Check hydration, these tired crip feet. Sometimes the I comes back online because of a proximity alert. That punisher is dancing too close. Repositioning protocol in effect. This time it's the heat.

It's winter outside, but these bodies burn enough sugars to heat a sauna. Pure, useless labor, churning out the excess of the world in the least harmful way we can make together.[13] Deploy fan. Swig water. Peel off the sequined top. That helps too. Fuck it, I pull my bra off over my head, tie it to the top, and tie both to silver rave bag. Pump back into movement to push the I back down into nothing. To lose this solitude, lose these lonesome cowgirl blues.

Then the I comes back to the fold, and I'm laughing, as I see Q, through the shag of textured limbs, over at stage right, with her tits out too, forearms raised, skinny fingers up, in that gyrating dance of hers. She sees me and we wave to each other. For twenty beats, the world belongs to us. The she and the me mix with the others, sequenced together. And the world is all we can feel.

Ketamine Femmunism

THAT WAS BEFORE COVID. Before COVID, this bitch got her rave on, locked back into the beat, built up her stamina, re-learned and elaborated her rave practices—only for it all to shut down. That bad dream year.

At 140 BPM a calendar year is 73,584,000 beats long. But some years, like some raves, have some weird duration. The "lockdown year" was like that. Was it a year? Or two? Is it still that same year? Nobody really knows anything other than that it is—or was—bad.[1]

That initial pandemic lockdown was hard in a special way on those whose sexual, emotional, and sensual needs are distrib-uted across a diagram of partial objects, such as those who go to raves or sex clubs. It trapped many, particularly queer and trans people, into something close to a one-to-one map between the property one rents and the interaction of the bodies in it.

Locked up in that isolation, a very dear friend chose to live in the past. The wake, on a rooftop, our tears freezing our faces.

This wasn't my first pandemic. It's happened before. A virus forcing us into the package deal of private property, family, solitude.[2] Suspicion, policing each other's need for touch. The loss of others through collateral damage from all that. I'm not advocating recklessness, but sometimes there's other risks alongside a pandemic. Some people don't do well without something like a communism of the flesh. Or, as I'll call it shortly, *femmunism*.

Particularly while it was warm, there were outdoor raves, what some ravers derided as plague raves. Some seemed like merely commercial enterprises. They were indiscreet. Never let your party be found by journalists who will sell you out for a byline.[3] Moral panic followed. Hard to deflect that when the event was for money in the first place. I went to none of those. I went to the other kind.

Hannah Baer: "Through the trees with frost beginning to crust on them, glistening in the moonlight, one of the friends drops a crushing track; a sample mutters, over and over, 'I am a nightmare walking.' I leave the dancefloor and wander around a falling down shed, behind the DJ. I am rolling, in a field where each blade of grass is sparkling with ice. The music sounds like a jet engine, a jackhammer, a machine gun. I am a nightmare walking. This forest fractured by strobe and side-chained 200bpm kick drum filter distortion filter distortion the new york bass that will break your face, and your face is freezing, frost on the trees everyone in all black, acid mdma s-ketamine r-ketaine adderrall psilocybin red bull black tea speed weed gummy reishi tincture I am a nightmare walking."[4]

The free raves too were controversial. Long discussion threads on Telegram, Signal, and Discord. Even in the cold of the first COVID winter—it got heated. Sometimes the worst kind of punishers don't act out, they call out.[5] They become cops about how everyone else acts. And yet beyond parasocial moralizing the talk kept verging on raving as a practice. What do we owe to each other? How can we become other than single beings? How do we find a space between the danger of the virus and the danger of isolation? This all called for some elaboration of rave practice.

We are not of that party that thinks the only danger to our health is the virus. We are of the party that knows this world is already out to kill us. That the habit-forming regime of work, consumption, family, and police kills too. With its casual violence, with its callous extraction. With its sorting and ordering of bodies, with many of our friends among the most disposable grades. We try to turn our attention to, not away from, those bodies even more disposable than ours. In the lockdown we try to make more, not less, of a gift of ourselves to others. Even if it just means a gloved hand giving a bag of food to a masked stranger.

Janus Rose: "The electric scooter is a crucial component in all this. When I stopped commuting to work, I started using it to deliver groceries to my neighbors through local mutual aid groups. When I arrived at one woman's door with shopping bags full of food, she expressed disbelief that I actually showed up, even though we had talked on the phone an hour earlier."[6]

But then: how to feed the body's other needs? The need to forget the self and become happy flesh, together. Street raves, no cover, donations for the DJs via QR codes. Punishers be damned. A DM from Q gives the location of the outdoor rave slash protest in Red Hook. We're on our way: T is driving us.

It's before she and I broke up, before I pull away from her world, into this one. By the time we're near, the location has moved to a dead-end street poking into the water, with a view of the Statue of Liberty, its white light far off and barely reading.

Later, when my Insta follow request is accepted, I see the flyer for this one: "Community solidarity. Rave as protest. Techno is Black music. Connecting is vital. Black lives more than matter. Utilizing music as our voice. Chaos can take shape in a new tomorrow. Please use this as a time to redistribute wealth for those who are in need. Masks and social distancing required."

Pretty words here. We all know they're not enough. But they're better than the ugly words, everywhere. We'll always be there, for what is now, defensively, an antifascism without guarantees.[7]

We're early. People are just arriving from the other site. A little grated drain in the cracked pavement attracts my attention. I get down on the ground and study it. Wafting up from the hole: the sound of the sea, rolling in and rolling out. Beneath the pavement, oceanic rave.

A is setting up the sound system, with N, Y, and Q assisting. Others fill a trash bin with mates and nutcrackers.[8] There's not enough ice. T volunteers us to go get some and refuse to take any money for it. We get two sleeves—sixteen bags. I'm feeling useful, shouldering a sleeve of ice through the crowd, although barely strong enough to hold it up.

The light fades over the water as Jasmine Infiniti takes the decks, here on this dead-end street. In the glint of the city, she stands in her own aura. A body, a self, its history. History as a scar. From it, she brings her own read. Nothing for it but to take the artificial dumbness of the machine and turn it out, make the machine spit chatter chitter, make it cum loud and hard over and over. That which does not kill us is still going to kill us, but we can make it make us dance to it for a while, for our need and pleasure.

Jasmine Infiniti: "The things that I have personally had to go through and that many other Black trans women endure, it's almost as if we are existing in hell already. It's kind of like, well if I'm already here, I might as well live it up and find the best parts of this existence that I can. It's about embracing that hell vibe. I want it to reflect that, but also have a little bit of sadness, a little bit resentfulness and a little bit anger, but also happiness and joy."[9]

T is dancing with me, to this joyful, bitter techno, at a rave, for the first time. It is like we just met. No memory. Y and Q and N appear and we're all pumping beats, stage right from Jasmine at the decks, where there's room for distance, and it's not too loud for T. I can see rave friends in the crowd: there's A and her girlfriend C, and V, who pops up everywhere. I think of the syzygy, just a few days ago, when Saturn, Jupiter, and the moon aligned in the sky. My stars align. My worlds feel each other's gravity in the booming void.

For this lateral eon, at least. But it will pull apart. Orbits decay. T and I will break up soon. Lose ongoingness. Wandering stars. For whom it is reserved: the black days, the dark days. 'Til new constellations form. But that has not happened, not yet. That story has yet to infect this situation with narrative's festering lack. This moment lacks for nothing.

Online to get offline. Chasing street raves is a way to rediscover the city, to find the texture of neglected junkspace. It's a way to turn the hellsites of social media inside out. In closed groups across various platforms, posters appear. It's like the old days, except there's no wheat paste.[10] Message your crew on Discord or Signal about which rave to chase across the city's ripped backsides. I pack my silver rave bag: water, bandana, cash, phone, some other supplies.

One time our little crew, C, Z, E, and me, crossed the Pulaski Bridge to a rail yard on the Queens side of Newtown Creek. The crowd had that psychotic energy. Anything could happen. There were people from all over the city, all scenes. There's a scrambling of the usual social diagrams in the moment between the end of the lockdown and the opening of venues. Nobody knows which party is for whom.

I'm with Z and E, as G split off with another crew. Later, I'll hear they were dancing in boxcars. We end up on the tracks near the sound system. It's hard to dance. The ground uneven. Ravers in the minority. Punishers pushing us out of their way. We sit on the tracks for a bit to plot our next move. Rumors of another party—under the other bridge.

A very young, very high, very drunk, very white cis woman stumbles and lands on us. She has lost her friends. (Some "friends.") She's disoriented. E tries to get her to drink water— first and most crucial act of care. She is confused and resisting. E looks at Z and me. This is not good. Our little crew is two clockable white trans women and one Black cis woman. The crowd around is mostly straight, white and cis. Could easily think the three of us are the problem here. Before we figure out what to do, drunk girl staggers off. I hope she gets home safe. We bounce just as the cops arrive.

But then there is that night at The Hole, as that little piece of street got named. It's cut in half there by railway tracks, with a footbridge over it. On one side, a fancy restaurant and brewery that makes organic mead. On the other, it's all warehouses and trucks, the pavement broken beyond repair. No beach beneath. It's Bushwick's junkspace zone—the kind of place modernity went to die. It seems fitting that this rave was thrown by an outfit called Regression. Big Ted Adorno would hate all this.

A slow start. It draws a straight crowd, and I came alone. Punisher walks right into my spot in front of the DJ and just stands there. He does a fist pump and a little jerky move, then pulls his phone out. I think of Kleist's essay on the marionettes.[11] Straight cis men can't dance without this self-consciousness. Can't let the beat take them. Can't dissociate out of their masculinity. There's exceptions, but then I don't think of those raver boys as straight when they're dancing.

I think about yelling at him. Or politely asking him to move, which just positions me as a useless girl. I decide he's not worthy of being in my presence and relocate. They can treat the situation like they own it, but we'll be gone. It's in our power to withdraw and leave them alone with nothing to feel smug about. I'm head-tripping on this for a bit, but there's L, there's Y, there's W, there's B. A and U show up. At some indefinable point, it gels. Take a bump. Get your motor on. Disappear into ravespace. Even straight men can get there, but only if they let the sound fuck them.

Rainald Goetz: "What had just happened, there must have been a rhythm to it. Because now all at once there came a break. And it exploded into an unbelievably thick electro beat, and the applause was frenetic, and everyone threw themselves into dancing. You practically got hurled upwards and battered by the bright, choppy party-frequency sensations and their rhythmic contrast, like a compositional element, to the offbeat pounding—an outright storm of musical bliss. What kind of track was this really? The feeling of consonance overwhelmed me and I was absolutely blessed. Effacement. Thankyou. Once more, while I danced, I had the most lucid thoughts about a theory of critique."[12]

Raving on molly is a problem at street parties, as they get shut down at random, and you can be left rolling for hours. The balance, already tilting, shifts decisively to ketamine. It's already popular with trans ravers. Dysphoria pushes a lot of us into dissociation, and k is a dissociative drug. Self and world disappear, and with them the friction between self and world, merging into the sonic shimmer mix.

The brain cops' only concept of dissociation is that to detach from this world must be a bad thing. But this world is broken. Even more than our bugged-out psyches. Maybe sometimes to dissociate can also be to "ressociate."[13] Why isn't that a word? That there's no words for where we go is maybe the sign that we're on our own, but on our own together, trying to find the ways we can endure the end of this world.

This need. The three forking paths I've found to get free. Ravespace: body and mind free from each other. Xeno-euphoria: mind submerged in flesh, chemically estranged into otherness. Enlustment: Let's talk about that one later.

I'm a lightweight with drugs, and that's why I'm still alive. I'm not interested in promoting them; they are a business like any other. I'm wary of them as metaphors, as some warmed-over romantic yearning for an outside. Maybe they can have a metonymic function, optional parts of a practice of making another city for another life, another body for another life.[14]

To make flesh here, inside this city, in the surround. In a time that reels off sideways. Let's call it *k-time*. Like the time of the k-hole. Folded into duration. This other time, k-time, happens only in the rave continuum. This k-time is not a messianic time, it's an imminent time. This k-time is not a time of duration, the romantic other of machine time.

Rather, it's machine time amplified to the moment where it splits from duration and takes the body into a sideways time, without memory or expectations, without history or desire.[15] A dissociative time, a transsexual time, a ketamine time. A time that's driven, a time of drives, a time without desire yet which still fucks. The time where together we might feel the presence of *ketamine femmunism*.

Sometimes when I'm raving, the theory sequencer kicks off on its own. Concepts dance in the sound. Into ambient awareness. Sometimes even into memory. It's more ludic than lucid. That's how I come to be thinking about what the late Mark Fisher dubbed "acid communism," and how it doesn't quite do it for me as critique, and these situations I've been writing here about raver practices allude to why.[16]

We're doing our best to socially distance while dancing, the streetlamps glancing off sweat-sheened flesh, their stalking light angling between the dancers, revealing. There's a pod of molly dancers near me, melting into each other. Making me think of acid.

Acid sometimes used to mean molly, or ecstasy—MDMA. I'm getting too old for that shit, but I still love that chemically assisted merge. Acid usually means LSD, which is back around again. But the solitary, contemplative head-trip points somewhere else than collective rave practices. Fine, go on your burner quest. It just has a romantic throwback tone that's maybe not the detour into the past most ravers want.

Acid is also a sound, and one that I really love, what Volvox played that time, that analog twist of the nipple. I ask Z, who is a technical girl, to describe acid in a sentence: "It's basically a resonant filter whose cutoff is driven by an envelope, manically sweeping it through the higher frequencies of the signal."[17]

Z helped me make my first acid track on her modular synth array. Helped me lace together the signal path, on its detour through the rack, a drift of electricity through this little city of noise. My track was terrible, as I did not know what I was doing, but danceable. I got up and danced, felt it in my body. Making the machine make me dance. This acid I want in this life.

There's something too retro about the desire for communism, as if it wasn't defeated, again and again.[18] It's a desire to live in a future to a past that history sliced off, leaving its scar. Capitalism mutated, as a virus will, into something worse. The desire for communism is a desire without the present, a sacrifice of life now to a time that did not and can now never come. It's a God that died, whom I still mourn.

What can still be shared, between humans and machines, between humans and humans? I wouldn't call it communism anymore. I lost faith. The word *femmunism* I got from a meme, which seems apt. The meme shows what I take to be a woman holding aloft a sickle crossed with a Hitachi magic wand. It's the queen of vibrators. It'll get you off when nothing else will. Pound you like no jack's hammer. It's the techno of orgasms. Femmunism is a subtraction. A sharing that includes the machine but not cishet masculinity, which is technically obsolete.[19]

I'll mention here, in passing, my fondness for Mark Fisher, for what I learned from his writing, and from him in person the few times we met. But the thing I want to take some distance from is the unexamined masculinity in both his aesthetics and politics. That the possibility he heard and felt meant letting go of a lot more than he was willing to discard.

The space of radical possibility might actually be with us vampires and other monsters in the k-time of the night.[20] That we're not alien to the proletariat but are always the part of it suppressed to cement the identity of the worker in subsumption to the family, nation, and state. Isolated from the possibilities of other relations of machine to flesh, flesh to flesh. The machinic puppet is the master, making us dance, leaving us strung out.

As Q says to me once, while we chill out, at a rave: "It's an avant-garde that people actually like." We are of that party experimenting with new machinic configurations, here and now. Not putting off to the revolution—that over the rainbow time—to do it for us. Our practice is here and now, sideways in time, in k-time.

We are the ones who had not just a theory but an art of happy flesh. Of how situations could be constructed, to stylize chance encounters of flesh, tech, sound, chemistry. We are the ones hacking our bodies, each according to their needs, refusing the alibi of nature as the mask of a mere arbitrary norm. We are the femmunists. Learning that the situations into which we can pool, in which we can let go of ourselves as private property, where we can let ourselves be fucked by beats, where men don't have to be "men."

There are men in ketamine femmunism—both trans and cis—who will let the beat fuck them. It's just not for the ones who stand around at the rave, not moving, on their cell phones, or critiquing the DJ's technique. It's for the ones who can dissociate out of the enclosed shell of their bodies, into the mix. They'll not regret coming through. I wish Mark had joined us.

4   **Enlustment**

NOBODY WAS SURE who organized it, but U was promoting it, and we trusted her that it would be cute.

The venue was a fifteen-minute walk away from my Bushwick apartment. I asked J to come with. Over DMs a few days before I told her that I like her and she said she likes me. Now I'm asking if she wants to meet me there or at mine or at hers. Not knowing where I stand.

Just the night before I ran into J at another rave. I'd been keen to see her. We had fucked that one time, and texted. And I thought we liked each other. Somehow it seems a lot easier to fuck someone a first time than to figure out if there's to be a second.

Always, I want there to be a next time. Unless it was really terrible, then I wish it had never happened at all. I have a problem with *ongoingness*. With wanting the story to have another season.

I talk to J when I run into her at the rave. We are on a little rise in the yard. I'm leaning into her. To connect, to find if the intimacy is still there, and because I'm hard of hearing.

We compare notes on kit. Her little black bag always has napkins. My silver one, a fan. That's when the other girl clocks us, comes over, looks at me coldly, looks at J and locks eyes. Gets her attention. Looks back at me, as if to say, not your girl, my girl. I'm dying.

What am I saying? J isn't anyone's girl. Only in my fantasy world of ongoingness might there be any more to her story where I might be in it. It's absurd, at my age, to imagine there can be much ongoingness at all. Particularly with one so young. The young ones look at me like I'm an alien creature.

Which I guess I am. I got to live as if there could be all sorts futures, and now there are hardly any at all. I don't blame them for saving any sense of ongoingness for each other. For treating me and mine as history. The lives I got to live are not part of their Bushwick dreamscape.

Kay Gabriel: "Walking down past a short wall or long bench where very many famous people with university jobs are sitting having lunch in middle school and McKenzie summons me down to the end, *Kay*, she says, *come meet Donna*, Mike says forget them they're at beauty cunt school and Harron says I can bring enough for the wedding."[1]

It's both an apt and inept word to use for a situation involving three trans women, but I feel cockblocked. Which maybe I deserve. I walk away. More dancing. There's house music elsewhere in the yard. My body will dance to anything. Dancing to house is great for getting into my body, if I can. It's pleasant when it connects my body to its past moments of living as a cis gay man.[2]

Only in this situation I felt my body was rotting garbage. I only stayed in the yard a little while. Inside on the main floor, Juana was DJ and it was going off, so it felt best to just pound every last neurotic insecurity out of me in the amniotic tide.

Theodor Adorno: "Listening has regressed, arrested at the infantile stage. Not only do the listening subjects lose, along with freedom of choice and responsibility, the capacity for conscious perception of music. They dissociate what they hear, but precisely in this dissociation they develop certain capacities which accord less with the concepts of traditional aesthetics than with those of football and motoring. They are not child-like but they are childish; their primitivism is not that of the undeveloped, but that of the forcibly retarded."[3]

After wearing the self down to a bare nub, time to go home. On the way out, some other girl takes my hand and holds it as I walk on by, as if to make me stay. Maybe I should.

I'd given away the second ticket to U's rave, somehow imagining that even though I'd already asked J to come with and she'd said yes, that she would not. I'd waited a while, 'til about 9 p.m. or so, then I gave it away. But now she's texting that she's coming, so I hit up the rave chat on Signal to find another. U sends a link for discount tix on Resident Advisor. Secured with a few clicks.

J is coming over, soon. A panic of wardrobe choices. It's cool. Summer, fading. So much for the "hot girl summer" meme of 2021. I'd barely got warmed up. The rave might be sauna hot, but it's cool out, and I'm feeling chilled. Sometimes my body temperature doesn't regulate too well. Or maybe when I'm nervous my body just amps up all the bad signals churning around, to find reasons to hide. This had improved a bit since I transitioned so I'm frustrated with feeling this old ganky way again.

I settle on a short, tight skirt in stretch-black and a tight, long-sleeve navy tee, boatneck, so it shows the straps of the plain black bra under. Padded: these tits need all the help they can get. Much consideration of footwear. The magenta Converse? Sheave on my black knee length Stuart Weitzman boots instead. I want to feel hot. I want to feel like someone could want me.

When J arrives, she flashes her winning smile. We hug, but she turns her head so I can't kiss her. The kissing had been so sweet, that one time. We'd done a bump of k which high-pass filters the senses but gives kissing a whole other slippery tone.

We crew up with Z and E. I take a picture of the four of us on the street before we head off. I wanted a souvenir. Of the moment, of all of us together. To remember when it started or when it ended. The ongoingness. It isn't clear.

The party is indeed cute, as they say around here. Generator outside. Strange that the building isn't powered. At one end, the DJ and speaker stacks, at the other, there's a makeshift bar, a low plywood shelf against the back wall, and a doorway, probably to toilets, shrouded in temporary black curtains.

I ask J if she wants a drink. Beer. Mate for me. I like the caffeine. Usually I don't dose it after 4 p.m. but it's a rave night, rave morning. We take our drinks with us onto the dance floor. The crowd is still thin so we can be wherever we want. Earplugs in, I head for the front of the stage. Like K it's where I like to be most.

Speaker demons, madison moore calls them: those who try to fuck the speaker, climb into it.[4] I'm a speaker demon, but to me speakers are switch. As a bottom by inclination, I would of course think it this way. I want to be fucked by sound. Not so much a sound that you hear, more a sound you feel.

Sandy Stone: "There's nothing like being massaged by a gajillion dB—we were made for this."[5]

Right up by the speaker, you can feel the air itself moving on your skin, fanning you. It's a little speaker demon trick. It will soon get wickedly hot in the room, but here there's a tiny breeze. An extra sensation, a tiny wind wicking on slippery skin.

Fire alarm—tripped by the fog machines. It's in a different tempo to the mix. A small worry if the fire brigade comes and brings the cops in their wake. I dance to the tempo of the alarm for a bit, but it seems too allegorical.

What makes illegal raves better than legal, V once said, is that they are illegal.

Can't help, even in the moment, having a theory about what I'm doing. The curse of being stuck in your own racing thoughts. Here's the theory of that moment: I want the situation, the entire situation, to fuck me. I want to be penetrated by light, fog, the floor, the walls, the anonymous swaying bodies. I want to be railed by pounding sound. Or at least, that's one mode of raving for me. I keep finding new ones and seeing those of others.

J comes over and shouts in my ear: "You like to be up front!" Wasn't going to deny it. She rips up a napkin and makes balls of paper to use as earplugs. "Have to get you some earplugs," I yell back. Make a mental note about it. I don't want her to be too close without good sound protection. Earplugs, or as I like to call them, rave condoms. I like to care for people. Maybe I just impose my idea of what they need. Ongoingness. I'm imagining we'll be around each other and I can gift.

Lost in k-time, opening into ravespace. Feel J near, but don't dance with her. J dances eyes closed, in an oscillating movement, head dipping, half smiling. Blissed out. Passing the vape by touch. I lose my balance if I close my eyes too long and like to be visually fucked by the scene anyway.

I'm not usually interested in dancing with just one person. You see couples dancing at raves. Can be annoying as they're lost to the other bodies around them. I'm not against it, just not interested in being too close to it. The sweet spot is little groups who let themselves ebb into each other and into the larger crowd around.

cranberry thunderfunk: "You can feel a viscosity when you wind your way through. An inexperienced or drunk crowd will be stiff, unaware of your presence, and hard to navigate. A seasoned crowd is easy to flow through even when densely packed. Picking the right spot in the crowd can be its own art."[6]

I'm attracted to J, and that shifts the relation in my body to the dance, moves it away from losing myself, more toward being in, and into, flesh. Autogynephilia is a cursed term.[7] As if it was a bad thing for a transsexual woman to be into her own body. To feel female embodiment as an intense kernel of expansive lust. It's ok for everyone else to feel that, but in trans women it was forbidden for a long time, and still suspect.

So steamy. I have to think about heat, actual heat, the regulation of the body as a heat machine, a metabolism. Heat pushing me into metabolic rift. I'm not usually spontaneous, so only after running a check with various parts of myself we take a vote and we're in: the solution to the heat is to take our top off and roll up our skirt. The top goes onto the bass bin, next to the now empty mate bottle. I'm down to black bra, roll of black skirt, and thigh-high black boots. And it feels hot, in every sense.

Layers of sensation, of lust and fatigue. Both just bundles of signals pulling in different directions. Lust keeps my body in itself, grinding. Fatigue is noise in that sensation, which some more task-oriented part of me is running through decision trees. Take a swig. Take a piss. Take a break. Kiss the girl.

I ask J if she wants water. We head to the bar. She gets a beer and I get water. I don't mind that I'm buying all the drinks but wonder what it means. She might make more money than I do. Most trans girls in New York are broke, but there's a few who make their weird brains command top dollar on the weird brain market, which is mostly but not only in tech.

Through the curtain to the toilets, pink-lit. We take a stall together to do a bump. I'm running low on the good-quality ketamine. I follow @dancesafe_ on Insta so I've heard about there being 2-FDC in the k. Pandemic supply chain problems, some say. This was a good baggie from N, a trusted source, so I feel ok sharing it.

Back in the nineties gay boys from the house music scene introduced me to k. Took me to church—to the Tunnel for Junior Vasquez's residency. Bumps of k kept us going. I was from a straighter techno rave scene and it wasn't common there. What fueled both was ecstasy—MDMA—before it was rebranded as molly. I'm getting too old for the comedown from that.

I used to do k off a key. J introduced me to the practice of using about three inches cut from a transparent straw. The straw that will end up in my kit used to be hers. The first time we fucked was at my place, and she left it. The learning of little everyday technics from each other.

She does a bump of heroic size. That much would put me in the k-hole, and I don't want to go there in a toilet stall. We talk for a while. Out of genuine curiosity I'm asking about her life. I have some of the story. I'm filling in blanks. It's not the standard nuclear family story, but then who has that?

One thing stands out, although I let it go in the moment. "Dancing helps me, helps with the damage," she says. I take this in, this gift, this way into her. I'll save it for later, if there is a later. I like to look for keys to people but not to intrude.

I can't help feeling like a teacher, which is after all not just my job but a core part of my being. I once sat down with a doll while Mithril beats pounded, to talk her through writing a book proposal. She was living discreetly in the back of a warehouse where she worked at the time, even doing sex work there. She had a great idea for a book. I don't know where she is now.

Not that I have anything to teach. More teaching in that sense of asking the questions that might help someone feel and think through something about themselves and the world. But I'm high and can't do it, and don't want that self here in the stall. I want to fuck J again. And I want these disparate selves—the ball of boiling lust, the reflective echo of teaching—to be as separate as possible.

I just say straight out: "I want to make out with you." With that little smile her face is on mine. Pressing me against the stall wall. I love to be pressed into walls and floors by bigger, stronger bodies. I used to associate this with femininity but that's a loose connection now. There is something about the coding of such situations making sense with the image this body has of itself, of its slightness, frailty. Its need to be pressed and held.

We break after a few minutes. J wants to pee alone. It's an interesting boundary about sharing stalls: who and when you can piss in front of another. I go to the mirror to fix my face.

I'm a mess. When matted with sweat you can see how my hair thinned. It's not pretty. Being taller, she could hardly have missed that. The face in the mirror clocking me is that of just another ageing, nonpassing transsexual. I tidy up as best I can. I'm confronted with the gap between a core confidence, connected to an outwardly expandable core of lust, and a rather shaky self-image, shot through with dysphoria. More k might take an edge off what I might feel about all that. The k hits, bright on bright.

Enough with the fraying, back to the fray! Dancing and k make it all go away!

We're up front again. I worry a bit about her unplugged ears, but have to turn off rave mom and trust her autonomy. The fatigue has kicked off a low-level endorphin buzz and the k is keeping the pain to a low static. We're past the opener DJ and the energy is ramping. Tonight I want to be rave bimbo. I don't care who is playing, or what. I just want to feel it.

I'm right in front of the horizontal bass bin that is in turn in front of the decks. The air pumped out of the speaker is going up my skirt. Roll the skirt up. Lose the top again. Drink water. Offer J water. A body of sound wraps itself around me, shudders through me, treats skin as if it's not there, viscera tricked 'til it sings. We're dancing on a sturdy wood platform suspended over the concrete floor. The platform is vibrating. I feel it oscillate up through my boot-clad legs.

The boots are a bit of an inconvenience, trapping hot air around my calves. It's a trade-off. I feel hot in a different way.

Anyway, more of my flesh is clothed in sweat than any garment. I turn to face the dancers. I don't make eye contact, as most are in their own dissociated state. I'm looking at feet or fog, or the lights above, or unfocusing to just register a flickering pattern. I feel the sound take me from behind. I can be seen and want to be. Queen of all she cares not to survey.

A tap on the shoulder. It's not J, it's what I take to be a young cis woman. She recognized me. Admires my writing. Read it in high school. High school! I ask her name twice but don't quite catch it. We shake hands. I'm aware of what a sight I must be, half naked and sweaty, hair a mess. Still kinda high. She stays to my right, dancing. It's fine but now I'm feeling self-conscious, stuck in my head.

Check in with J. We need water. A break seems timely. Back through the crowd. A gentle passing of a particle through a field, minimal disturbance.

I get us another round of drinks. Look for a place to chill. We could go outside, but the darkness in here appeals. It's a situation with the possibilities of the moment. We settle into the plywood shelf at the back. Memories of the plywood under me when Edward fucked me at a rave twenty-odd years ago. Enlustment can have topological folds, and k-time can run across the folded surface.

There's a speaker right behind us so it's too loud to talk. I feel the wood under vibrate as I lie next to her, shaping myself into the plywood and the length of her body. Rest the feet, replenish liquids, press this sweat-slicked body next to hers. She doesn't pull away.

I'm not spontaneous. There's always delay. There used to be a lot of delay. It's only since transition that I can express what is not even a desire. It's this enlustment. It's not a lack in the self, looking for an impossible object. It's an excess, an overflowing of the body. It's energy pushing out. I'm a bottom, sure, but pushy with it. Maybe aggressive, even. I'll come back to that.

Four beats, then the move. Now I'm straddling her hips, hands pressed to the plywood, pressing my mouth on hers. And she responds. The way she kisses—so luscious, exploratory, lively. A little biting. I can't quite figure out how to bite back, unable to think. Two live wires twisting, shorting, becoming something sparky and hot-wired.

Vaguely aware we're attracting onlookers. I have exhibitionist tendencies, so that just feeds me. In the dark, I'm just thin white flesh, the shape interrupted by the horizontal black bar of the bra, the rolled up black skirt over black panties, probably showing now—and the verticals of long black boots. I love how the boots feel. They cover my crip feet and I forget about them.

Pressing into her, grinding on her. From on top, while kissing, it's hard to use your hands. Anyway, I'd rather be touched than be touching for a minute. To be as little as possible that's not body.

I get in my head while making out sometimes. I strategize. I think about switching positions, think again. Sixteen beats pass. Now. Roll her on top. Feeling selfish. Taking what I want. Wanting only the present. Forgetting all about ongoingness.

Her weight is on me. Feeling her thigh, its firmness, length. She is not only taller but a lot stronger. Feeling her breast. Small—not long on estrogen. Sometimes you have to go gently on those. I'm pressing her ass against me.

Hard beats thump through her body and through the plywood her body grounds me against. This is lust, not desire.

It's situational. In this situation, this little oil slick of space and time, this is what bodies want. Two bodies press outward from each other into each other. The contact surfaces become a thing in itself. For a while, then it is over.

For a moment—how many beats?—this other dissociated state, of enlustment. That enfolding bloom of lust, extruding out of bodies, toward each other. Detached from past or future, expanding into hot time. It's not like xeno-euphoria, into the cool otherness of xeno-flesh. It is into the sludgy banality of the mammalian body.

She wants to stay only a bit longer, until three, and then go home. We're at the back of the room this time. I don't think she's a front-of-the-room raver, and it's good to mix it up. We find a convivial spot in the crowd for a while. A sphincter in time opens and swallows us up.

On our way out, B greets me. I give him a hug. Y is sitting on the ticket table. Kisses. She told me only yesterday not to go after girls so young. I'm feeling a little sheepish. I text her: "Don't judge me lol." Outside we meet Z and E. Stories: Some creep followed E around, trying to buy her a drink despite her firm refusals. Z finally told him off.

The four of us walk away. I'm aware that J is holding her distance. I've been ignoring signs, registering only those I want. The ones that made me feel that the situation had an opening toward desire, toward ongoingness. The taste of mutual enlustment was there. This flesh met that flesh. But what wasn't there was any sign from her that responded to my more generic desire, that this lack in me, this other hollow, could even for a moment be fulfilled in a way that signaled ongoingness. I'll be waking up alone again. We say goodbye at the corner.

Z and E wait just a little ways off. I catch them up. E wants fries, but there'll be nothing nearby open this late, or this early. I offer to make something. E does one of her brilliant post-rave reviews. I say she should do a blog, and Z instantly agrees. It's not lost on me that two white trans women who other white people used to treat as men are encouraging a Black cis woman to just do a thing that she'd be good at. To not think twice, to follow an impulse. We come from different stories. Different promises of ongoingness.

I'm thinking of going back alone to that rave all through the meal that E makes for us, but I'm tired. I'm feeling that sweet exhaustion that is one of the best things about raving. The body just giving in. Not before I order some good-quality audio earplugs online as a gift. Ongoingness.

The next morning, J texts me. "I'm sorry I don't want to be sexual anymore. I do want to be friends!" My whole mood drops. I'd been living in the fantasy of a desire. That someone would fill a small part of a lack. If only every now and then, if only for a little while. One should not hope for things, least of all ongoingness.

I take a while to respond. I'm trying to be cool, but I get pissy. Then regret it. Then I think about what good rave crew she is. I'll ask her to go dancing again, not soon but someday, but just for the dancing. And I want to know about her damage. That's what friends do, right? Friends know about our damage. Friends have each other's keys. Even rave friends, who can be intense but temporary.

What's to really be wanted, or needed? The rave need not be a space of desire at all.[8] Just a space that might open sometimes toward enlustment. But lusts edge onto aggression, violence, unboundedness. That creep who followed E around. Was I a creep? Did I press on this girl too hard? Oh no! I made a bold move. I thought the signs were clear. In the sober morning, I still think they were. All she said is there's no ongoingness to that. As there really isn't to many things at all.

A rave is just a pocket in time in which there's more time. But the pocket closes, and spills us out, and then that was all there was.

I'm trying to write about practice, about practice in a situation. A situation is not a story. The thing about autofiction as a kind of writing is that if it's honest, stories never really end with the happy ever ongoingness. Something always dies. Even if just a flicker of useless desire.

Maybe this is an age in which to become disinterested in our own desires, as they always live in the future, and there's not much of that. What we have is the sideways time of the now, a latent destiny. A time for which the rave is the aesthetic form, a metonymic part.

I'm writing, furiously, alone in my bed. About J, about that rave. For no reason, or maybe just as a reason to pass through this sadness. A tear splats on the keyboard. I've not been able to write since I transitioned, so it feels good to feel bad about it all while writing.

Phone buzzes. It's Margret. She texts to ask me about doing a book for this series on practices that she edits. Giving in to a manic impulse I say yes if it can be this: *Raving*. But how to write a book about raving as practice that is itself a rave practice? Usually, one writes for a future, for ongoingness. A rave just goes until it stops. Sometimes when the police arrive.

I was texting my friend Eva Hayward about it all morning. I don't know if some of these lines are hers or mine. A good conversation is also a rave that way, the blending, edgeless dance. It goes and then stops.

Problem with being human these days is that our subjectivity never adds up. The subject is always split, always divided, feels it lacks. You can spend years in therapy working through that. Or become a raver. Get out of your head, merge into k-time. Take some hard lefts. Drives go off in at least three directions: ravespace, xeno-euphoria, enlustment.

Maybe there's still more kinds of dissociation one can practice. Practice, like an art. Maybe dissociation could be its own aesthetic category.[9] Not specifically a trans thing but something at which we're virtuosos.

Sometimes rave dissolves brain into body, liquid self evaporating on a hot core of enlustment, to be pressed and prodded by sound, by this gloriously hot other body. Sometimes there's ravespace, an easier dissociated state to get into for me. To not be there at all. No self, no body. And then sometimes xeno-euphoria takes over, a chemical strangeness, covered in writhing tentacles.[10] Having found these variations on raving practice— maybe there's more. No point desiring them. If they're to be had, they happen.

At the rave, in any of these states, there's just the situation. As with writing, in any of its states. When there's just the situation of language itself. No ongoingness. Like the rave, writing is a practice where I can go and get free, of dysphoria, of sadness, of useless desire. The work is the cum stain of its inception.[11]

Resonant Abstraction

WHAT KIND OF WRITING IS THIS? What kind of reading turns
on having a genre to put it in? Am I a journalist, a novelist, an
ethnographer, a documentarian?[1] Any of those would bring a
practice from without and submit raving to its discipline.

I want a practice of writing that is more adapted to the rave
situation, even if it has to be adapted from my other practices.
The discipline of indiscipline, as the anarchists say. A scholarly
practice of pleasure, of play, that opens to expansive need, in
selves and others.

I throw myself into experiences, felt as sensations, parsed
as perceptions—out of which might emerge concepts.[2] Let's
think of concepts as *resonant abstractions*. Like diagrams,
they gather perceptions into fields, patterns, rhythms, under
a name. A name that will now work more like a chord than a
note in a sentence. Resonating with concordant perceptions,
of the surround.

The practice of writing, I have to disclose, comes in not only after raving, but before. Even if raving comes from a need to get out of myself, it's still a particular self: an old white coworker, who is crip, queer, trans—and a writer. So many particularities. The concepts abstract from those particulars, toward other particulars with which the concept may or may not resonate. If a concept doesn't resonate with your particulars, make another, in practice.

I choose terms for this writing, this practice, that are derided and ridiculed—autofiction and autotheory, as they are to genre what we trannies and faggots are to gender: not to be taken too seriously.[3]

From the autofictional writing of perceptions, then, to an autotheoretical writing of concepts. But with the general proviso that the *auto* that writes doesn't add up. It will be a mix, some part auto and some part allo, other, and more interestingly, part xeno—invitingly strange: xeno-flesh. Just fluctuating bundles of feelings and thoughts. And with the rave-situational proviso that what the auto needs most of all is moments when it can dissipate itself, not be there, pare down to a moving part or floating notion.

Let's put these unkept filaments of thought and feeling, matted together as this writing, this writer, into a field of others.[4] Don't worry if this is confusing. I can barely follow it myself:

Raver X was tight with raver Y and with raver Z, but Z and Y had a falling out. X remains friends with both. Z is friends with raver C who hates Y, friend of X, who is neutral about C. X is friends with A, who is friends with X, Y, and Z but dislikes C. Y is friends with B, who is friends with X, Y, and Z, but has had a falling out with A.

Had to draw a little diagram to figure that out. Diagram: line writing. I drew a diagram of ravers around me, imagining them as buzzing atoms in some unstable chemical compound. Then I put another piece of paper over the drawing and traced it, like when I was a kid, changing some lines, making a slightly different diagram. This is actually that different one. This "diafiction" might convey some of the texture of lines and nodes in a queer and trans raver macromolecule. Let's braid this diagram, this tracing of a corner of raver connections, into a larger weave.

This diagram might overlap with others. Let's say that C is in love with D who used to be friends with Y, but X hardly knows D and doesn't know anything about their presence on other diagrams. E is the lover of Z and is somehow still friends with practically everyone. X goes raving with F, who only knows any of these ravers through X. F attempted to have sex with X's roommate, until X asked F not to and F agreed to that boundary.

Diagrams back onto others. X and Z have both had M couch surf with them, and X may have bought ketamine from her to avoid having to go to N because N is close to Y, with whom X is still friends but is maintaining some mutual distance. Also: M likes men, whereas most of the trans women in the main diagram like women. The dolls' diagram and the lesbian trans girl diagram don't connect all that much.

Some of the breaks of connection are random. Some may involve allegations of bad behavior.[5] There may be attempts at formal mediation about those allegations by other parties. Those mediations are confidential so I'll say no more. As to what is private and what is public—that's complicated. X, Y, D, Q, and Y were present at the rave where Z and E fell in love with each other, rolling in the yard while the others drank water and X shared tangerine slices.

Several ravers out of sorts with each other are nevertheless on the same Signal or Discord. People show up at the same clubs, parties, and raves. Z did not go to one because Y would be there, but X did, and talked to both Y and to H, who has been a bit inappropriate with Z. Then X got friendly with J, who lives with Y, despite Y telling X that the mutual attraction between X and J is probably a bad idea.

Diagrams map onto other diagrams. X became friends with G through Z and E. They hung out one time, even though G is estranged from X's friend Y. Then G informed X that there's been an exposure to COVID, probably at a rave, so both had to get tested, self-isolate, and inform others in this diagram and in other diagrams.

This diagram life is not really all that unusual among urban millennial queer and trans people of some means and proximity to whiteness. The separation of publicness and privateness are constantly renegotiated within shared households and among networks of various kinds of love and sex, sometimes polyamorous. Lots of ravers also DJ or host club nights, and pull from diagrams in which they are nodes to their shows. And while to buy weed you just text and a courier comes, ketamine and molly are more a connection through the diagram.

The diagram expresses itself in situations but also through styles of connection on social media.[6] That may have layers, from public accounts to alts on Twitter, finstas on Instagram, and the restricted lists users can set up for stories using the "close friends" feature. Then there's Signal, Telegram, and

Discord groups. Or group chats: for example, X, Y, Z, O, and E maintained a group chat all through the 2020 COVID lockdown.

Two things make this and connected diagrams stylistically specific. One being the relations of obligation and mentorship of trans people, particularly of trans women. For example, among the trans women in the diagram A has been out the longest. Q, X, Y, Z, and V have feelings of respect for A, even if they were not mentored by her. The other being that there are raves in which everyone is likely to bump into everyone, on the floor, in the toilets, in the chill-out space, if there is one.

At the rave, friends can have a special style of relation: intense, joyful, but of the moment. It's a style that can have intensity without ongoingness. If someone leaves the scene they may not be remembered for very long. Raver nemeses, on the other hand, create frictions that catch and burn those around them.

These ravers live in Brooklyn. Mostly in Bushwick, some in neighboring East Williamsburg, Bed-Stuy, or Ridgewood. The latter is technically in Queens but in psychogeographic terms feels like Brooklyn.[7] The raves are also mostly in Brooklyn, wherever there's slightly neglected light industrial junkspace.

Before the pandemic there was a great little venue opposite a scrap metal yard, so far into Ridgewood it might as well be in Maspeth, which really does feel more like Queens. It held only about thirty people. Scene of two great nights, one featuring a live set from January Hunt, the other from DeForrest Brown Jr. Various ravers were at one or the other or both. And as always, rave friendship traces a fragile line over chasms of race and class.

January Hunt: "I have a lot of conceptual ideas and name identities, but it's hard to devote myself fully to any of them.

It likely has to do with the feeling of being malleable in a body, and wanting to stretch that infinitely. I didn't go to college. It's been hard to take myself seriously without institutional backing to help cement my identity as a creative person. It has always felt like survival came first and anything else was a hobby or a pastime and trying to imagine combining these things has always felt complicated. I wish I could comprehend that when I was younger, but growing up without a financially stable home ingrained in me that you had to prioritize making money to survive."[8]

January was in the same artists' group show as T. I met January briefly at the opening. I got her number from our mutual friend Torrey, and we met for coffee one time. Then I started seeing her around at raves. We link through three diagrams here, starting with the art diagram T is on, to which I'm also connected. Then there's the white trans girls of Brooklyn diagram: I got on that thanks to trans women reaching out to me via social media after I came out. Then there's the rave diagram.[9]

DeForrest I met after I bought a skirt from a company that his partner runs with W, who works bar at some raves. DeForrest made an album with Bergsonist that's partly derived from their reading of one of my books.[10] Here's yet more diagrams: a big one to do with fashion and artisanal production in Brooklyn, and a little one to do with my books and how they circulate among people of a certain class. Ravers as an immanent class, as Nick Bazzano ventured: those collected by this raving labor that produces nothing but itself.

Back to the rave continuum, to those shows in the Maspeth-seeming side of Ridgewood. Both January and DeForrest were "live." January brought some modular synth components and improvised in real time. DeForrest uses computer-based software that emulates the signal processing of modular synths. Either way, it's both like and unlike jazz. It's like jazz in being about the artist playfully pushing a machine to its limits, only it is about machines that process electric signals rather than metal tubes or metal wires vibrating in the air. It's unlike jazz in that the machine can automate the production and repetition of a sound in time, theoretically forever—virtual k-time. It automates the repetition of signals, as so many twenty-first-century technologies do.

DeForrest took a break in the middle of his own set to step outside. The machines played on; the ravers danced on. The styles of both the social diagram and the aesthetic practices in these situations lace together with contemporary technics. What's interesting to me about both the artists and the ravers is the improvisation, of sound, of life, within the affordances of these machines.

In the music, at the rave, in social life, there's play in and against a borough-wide studio designed really for nothing other than extracting a style-surplus out of our collective needs and drives—*style extraction*.[11] We play, make moves, gestures repeating, becoming styles—that are extractable as forms of intellectual property, harvested for the benefit of a ruling class that owns and controls the vectors of information. Within our little shifting diagrams, we do our best to evade capture, and if captured—get paid.

On a good day, or night, or morning, the play between us, that is the us, constructs situations of and for femmunism, in a k-time that slides out from and into the gap between the times of body and machine. So pretty when that happens! Tactics for temporary release from commodified information, but which can be captured in the Bushwick wilds and tamed back into the commodity-style. Into this book, for instance, LOL. The urban style-extractor has become a social type.[12] One rich for satire.

Macy Rodman: "Have I not seen you since I got back from Berlin? Oh my god that was so crazy. It was honestly life changing. Like I'm probably going to move there like 90% sure. Like, it's like one big Bushwick. Like I met this drug dealer who, by the way, had the best shit I have ever done. Like I don't even know what it was called. Drugs don't even have names over there. It's just like just do it with whoever and trust that it's gonna like be this amazing experience and it always is. It's like this insane mixture of coke and ketamine or I don't even know. So I met this guy and we ended up spending three days together. We were at Bergheim for 24 hours. Finally we went to sleep and he convinced me to stay the rest of the month and I was like yeah ok and then he was like you should do this installation art thing and I was like yah totally! And so I created this installation in this abandoned mall and it ended up in *Artforum*, randomly, like my first thing that I tried. So I'm like honestly going to move there I think I can get like a teaching gig or something and apartments were literally like a hundred dollars a month there. So I gotta figure some stuff out here but honestly, why not? I just gotta ask my mom but she'll probably be cool with it."[13]

In a New York that runs on extracting surplus information of all kinds, "Bushwick," as a sub-ambience of "Brooklyn," names the psychogeographic zone where agents of harvest and capture retrieve aesthetic stylizations from free play and turn them into intellectual property.[14] The real estate here has value because of the improvisation in new flavors of information and connection that percolate through it, of which the rave scene is just one instance. Whatever actual jobs, if any, ravers have, we're also at work producing styles for life inside the machine.

Improvising our lives together is an art that takes commitment or training. Of those on the raver diagram, and on the connecting diagrams that I know, only two did not attend college. They became the beautiful ravers they are through immersion. Those with degrees are more likely to have regular white-collar jobs in design or other style-commodifying trades, such as H and L, while V works for a Brooklyn-based media company famous for extracting and selling Brooklyn as style.

Others work in tech, including Z and J. Some teach, mostly adjunct, such as F and R. Some are in social services around queer sexual health. Some are in mental health care. Some work in nightlife, as do A and N. Some are sex workers. Some sell ketamine. All except for me range in age between mid-twenties M and mid-forties H.[15] Most are white. Some are trans. Most would be fine with being described as queer.

As it is where value is experimentally produced and stylized, Brooklyn is expensive. Everyone has a roommate or three. There's few private moments. Hanging out with F in her rent-controlled living room, just getting to know her, when her cis roommate started pottering around in the kitchen behind us. F invited me into her room. Won't describe her private space. That night, every time I left this little sanctuary, F reminded me to close the door behind me, to keep the ambience in.

The only private space she and I ever had, besides her room or mine, was a club toilet.[16] She sat to piss while I fished in my silver bag for ketamine and that straw. After bumps she left so I could lock the door again and piss alone.

H is Brazilian, S is Russian, B is Australian. Except for V, few of the Americans are born New Yorkers. I'm not the only one who came to Brooklyn from all over because it seemed to be a great machine for producing styles of life. To drift the streets, unknown to everyone. A stranger among strangers.

At least on a good day. But there's what H calls the queer tax to pay. We have to gather here to feel alive, relatively safe, among our people, but we pay for it. Only relatively safe: As I write, rumors circulate about two stabbings in the vicinity of two clubs frequented by queer and trans people. (Later, as I copyedit, the news is that an arsonist destroyed another club—fortunately nobody was killed). For queer and trans people, particularly if they aren't white, Brooklyn is still not any kind of home. Which is why there's nightlife. Another city for another life, but already immanent to this city, in its shadows.

Juliana Huxtable: "I'VE MET NEARLY EVERYONE I KNOW AT NIGHT. A TIME/PLACE AMONG THOSE WHO SIMULTA-NEOUSLY LIVED WITH AND IDOLIZED EACH OTHER WITHOUT MOURNING DECADES PAST. A PLAYGROUND OF CAREER AES-THETES, QUEENS (OF ALL VARIETY), CRITICALLY-INCLINED CURMUGEONS-WHO-WRITE, INTERNET PERSONALITIES, AND ARTISTS WHOSE WORKS I ONLY SAW AS PROPS IF AT ALL— YOUNG AT HEART IF NOT IN SPITE OF YEARS ACCRUED."[17]

Nightlife is a liminal situation on the edge of the daytime city, with its ambivalent anonymity—one that is also under constant if more discreet surveillance.[18] One night a small group including X, Z, C, and M went to see their friend K play an ambient set at a fancy Manhattan venue in an übergentrified area. Waiting outside the mall-like structure. Stares from finance bro coworkers. C was already pretty far gone. Puked in one of the planters. To the others, edibles seemed advised. X, Z, and M overdid it. So much so that M had a panic attack and left the venue. X and Z texted to see if they should come out too for support, but M was fine just walking around.

After the show C took charge of the march back to the subway and so fucked it up the whole group got thoroughly lost. X made them stop for water and snacks while Z took over on directions. It was a fun evening—everyone chattering on as the party drifted through the streets—until Z got them to the Penn Station subway.

Three cops by the turnstiles. Three cops on the other side. Three cops in the center of the platform. Three cops at the leftward end. The little band of queer and trans ravers instinctively headed for the other end of the platform—where there were yet more cops. Most of the cops were on their phones. A few gave the hard cop-stare.

These (mostly) white queer and trans people might prefer those slippery zones of Brooklyn nightlife. There's still cops. There's still potential violence, on the street, even in the venue. It just feels more like the surround. But safety is relative. The idea of a "safe space" probably came from the ballroom houses.[19] There's nightlife workers doing an important job trying to make clubs and raves safe spaces, but the rave can never be utopia. Just a more conducive situation.

Not least because it takes money to live close enough to nightlife that you can take your chances walking home in the morning. That's if landlords will have you. M is a young white trans woman. She has money, made from sex work and selling ketamine. She is also a magnificent DJ, although money from that is cash as well. If she can find a studio apartment with a discreet entrance her businesses will flourish, and she can continue to play the stock market. M has viewed dozens of apartments with several brokers. Some will not even give her an application form. And this was during the lockdown, when for once rents dropped as the vacancy rate was high.

The hard part is to acknowledge the small but undeniable role rave culture plays in gentrification. Ravers cluster in proximity to rave and club venues, many in former light industrial districts. Hardcore ravers and other kinds of dedicated nightlife people create situations that attract coworkers, who move into the same areas, driving up the rents, edging out other kinds of tenants, usually nonwhite working-class people.

P. E. Moskowitz: "Then, without warning, the notices showed up under the door. Soon after, two men appeared at the building. They pushed their way into Genetta's apartment and asked to see her bedrooms. She could tell they were assessing how much every apartment might be worth. She couldn't tell much else: the men told her their names, their company had no website. A few weeks later, official-looking forms started arriving from the duo's LLC. One said the tenants had to reapply for their apartments. Another claimed each apartment owed $7000 in back rent. They noticed new security cameras in the building, pointing not at the hallway but directly at each tenant's door. This would usually be the point in the story when tenants, not knowing their rights, start leaving."[20]

As most coworkers wearily know, New York is a city of maximum extraction. Not only will most jobs entail the estrangement of the labors of your heart and soul as well as your body—so will your (few) nonworking hours. You are supposed to be tweeting and 'gramming and otherwise hustling all aspects of your being.

That there seem to be muted signals emanating from another world, a nightlife world, where hot and cool aliens play, has a special appeal. Nightlife, rave centered or otherwise, is hardly exempt from style extraction. It was partly through being a face in nightlife that Q ended up working for a very hip Brooklyn fashion label. But it can appear so, or be dreamt of as so, by coworkers with CDJs gathering dust in the corner of a bedroom in some shitty shared apartment.

Raves have a particular place in the fantasy life of coworkers—and here I should acknowledge that I'm a coworker myself. I have a day job and the times I can dance through from doors to closing are rare. Besides freeing me from gender dysphoria, raves also free me from alienated labor—or appear to. Techno pounds the living shit out of my brain, freeing it from nagging worries about emails unsent. The psychic damage of certain kinds of cognitive and affective labor can be temporarily healed on the dance floor.

I see Jack Davis across the dance floor, and discreetly wave. I avoid students and most know to avoid me. At a rave, I'm off the clock, and so are they. Then I remember Jack just graduated. Wave, smile, head on over, hugs and shouted greetings. We head for the chill-out space in the yard.

Turns out we avoided each other at a lot of the same raves. Jack offers up the theory that, far from being the overcoming of individuality by merging into the beat, raves allow "dividual" parts of bodies a free space.[21] I agree. Maybe it's where parts of selves detach from their fictional wholes but also can reach out to other partial parts and connect.

Queer rave culture is then a diagram not so much of people as of dividuals. A diagram of partial connections and disconnections, mapped onto a slice of the city, which is in turn a site of rent extraction. Which, in turn, many ravers have to pay for by renting out their minds and bodies to various style-extraction industries so that they can afford to live in proximity to the rave, but which means eventually that they'll drive it away. The rave can never escape the totality of maximum extraction, of styles and of rents. It can offer partial moments, interior to it, yet off the clock—unclockable by it.

How does anyone know there's such a thing as queer raves anyway? I had a guide in Q, who took me by the hand. How does anyone else know? Brooklyn, with its shared households, clubs, and itinerant raves, has its double in the disintegrating spectacle of social media: Instagram accounts, some public, some not. Some run by promotors, some by DJs, all of whom have their followings. Then there's certain email lists. One party, very old school, has a private Facebook page.

There's pressure on promotors to get crowds who will buy enough tickets to exceed outlays. But that means a random assortment of coworkers and punishers, which will drive away the ravers who need it, whose presence is part of the attraction in the first place. While DJs might not want to hear it—the crowd is what makes the rave. For a crowd to get off, to really be a rave, the crowd needs to be seeded with a goodly proportion of actual ravers who really know how to dance.

Then there's the club kids. They need nightlife, like ravers do. But they go to be seen and see each other rather than to lose themselves. Club kids and ravers both need nightlife, although their needs pull against each other.

Geoffrey Mak: "The scene was clubby, queer, and messy. It had a diversity I hadn't found in the literary world. At the club, people were identified by their race, sure, but more by their look, their attitude, their drama, their performance. It was about surface, but it was not superficial. I loved the scene, and loved it hard. If, at sex parties, my race made me invisible, I found the opposite to be true at the club. It was important for me to learn how to dance, because I demanded to be seen. When the strobes came on, I pretended not to notice people watching. It was exhilarating, because nowhere outside the club did I ever command this attention. It was the height of the culture wars and I had learned how to vogue, which I found funny and passive aggressive. Whenever people asked me at the club if I was voguing, I would say I'm not appropriating anyone's fucking culture, I'm doing Tai-Chi. Obviously, I was carrying."[22]

Hardcore ravers need a lot of hours on the floor, but they're still selective about where they'll go. They need good DJs, sound and light, and sometimes most of all to be free from punishers. They're aware that they are part of what makes a cute rave. Promotors might make some "list" so they're in for free. Or there might be links to discount tickets offered in closed groups before the public release. Or there's reparative discrimination at the door. To make space for queer and trans people who need it and can handle their habits. A good door bitch knows through observation and practice who to wave on in and who to keep out. Who will bring their energy and who would just suck.

Some raves have a no-photo policy, some don't. I'm at one that is serious about no-photo, taking a break on a banquette near the door. I look over at the person reclined full-length, sacked out, on another banquette. It's a very tall and slender woman, clutching her phone to her breast, dead to the world, and in flawless makeup. Not just tall, I'm thinking, but a "tall girl," a trans woman. Then I recognize her: one of the top trans models currently working. I reach for my phone for a picture. . . . and stop.[23]

This rave has its own hashtag, which is mostly pictures of ravers before or after the party, in their pretty outfits and makeup, or trashed in the morning light. That what happens in between is mostly invisible is part of its charm. It's a good party, or it was, and I'm not the only raver who has had magical moments there. The invisibility creates a kind of aura. As if the absence of reproducible images pointed to something with special provenance. Only not so much to its presence in history, in tradition, as its near-complete absence.

It won't last. Parties lose their aura, ongoingness, get replaced by others. The pandemic lockdown took some big promoters out, and some upstarts gained a reputation with some good free street raves. New DJs come up. Venue scouting is an art, and sometimes new promoters, seeing the borough with fresh eyes, spot new potential situations.

Often what kills it is the style extraction. Which inevitably starts with blackness, the most hauntedly auratic zone of situations—and also the one that can be harvested with maximum exploitation, particularly if it's Black and queer and trans. The ballroom scene has been picked clean, from Madonna to *Paris Is Burning* to *Pose* to *Legendary*.[24]

A rave is temporary. A passage of a few people through a rather brief moment in time. Some things about it as a practice happen in the time of the situation and maybe belong there rather than in writing. So I left them there. And while a rave is temporary, raving is outside of time. The rave continuum goes sideways in k-time, until it mutates into something else. Until the end of the world.

madison moore: "The floors in queer nightlife spaces are a wet, hot, sweaty netherworld, where the bathroom floor might be caked in sweat and soggy toilet paper, and where as you move through the venue you might be wading through an elixir of haze, spilled boozed, glitter, crushed drink cups and cans, straws, cum, poppers, metro cards, debit cards, bills, coins, tiny drug bags, lighters, dirt, cigarettes, loose tobacco, and rolling paper."[25]

Some of the graceless traces a rave expels back into the world will last a long time. The ongoing scar of Anthropocene dirt. The aluminum water can, for a hundred years. A ketamine baggie, a thousand years. A glass mate bottle, maybe a million years. Landfill as archive. Where this book will end up as well.[26]

Gavilán Rayna Russom: "The body and the land hold information. They hold the past and the future as they exist in the present. The land and the body know they have been colonized, they also remember when this was not the case and they know that one day they will no longer be colonized. Just like the memories held in the drum break and the objects held in the museum, as we talk and work and dance and live, innovating social frameworks, making meanings, reclaiming ancestral relevance and affirming sustainability, they will one day be free and they will speak, and we will listen, or we will become extinct."[27]

Techno began as the sound of blackness giving itself a future in the ruins.[28] What did it become? At worst—well, I don't want to get into that. At best—a machinic, sonic time that can be endured. An endurational time, k-time, for a period in which durational time is no longer available to us. A trans time, with no future, yet which makes a present of the present. The gates to paradise are locked. It became private property. But we can go round the back and hop the fence.

7

8

9

10

11

17

18

EXIT

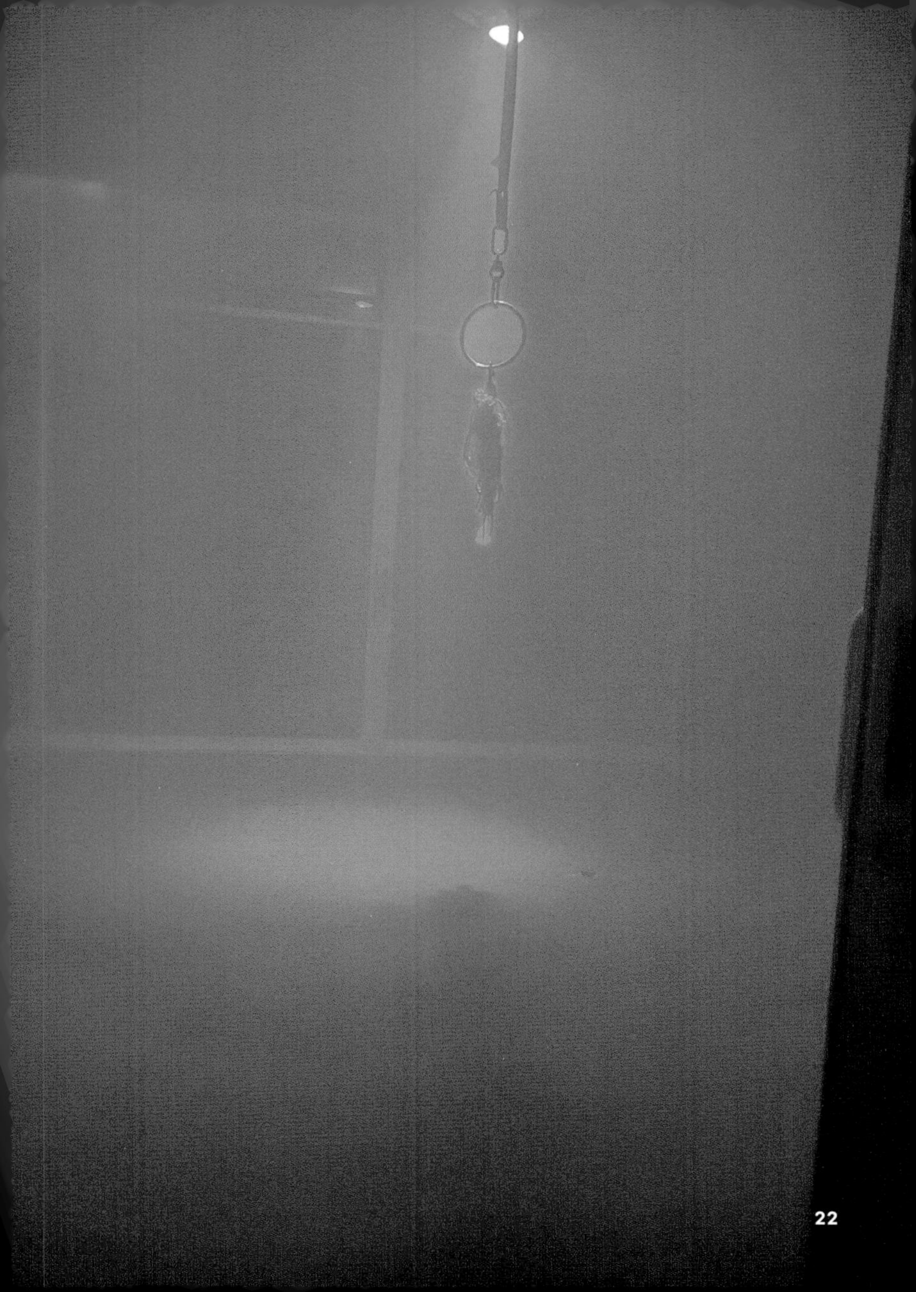

24

25

THESE LINES CAME TO YOU from my bed, where I do much of my writing. You were next to me in it, writing on your own laptop, working on your novel. I don't know what the best thing is that we do together here: fucking, sleeping, talking—or writing. They're all good. Although it makes me a little anxious watching you now, here again, as you read this, and write, in your squiggly hand, in my margins.

I was going to write you into this story in the third person, but I've run out of letters to give ravers in place of names. Anyway, you didn't come from the rave scene. I looked for you. I was on eight dating apps. Nine, if you count Twitter.

At a used bookstore, I walked the aisles looking for any-thing, round and round the crammed shelves, until finally my hand was pulled to a book of love letters I'd never heard of in the last aisle. This one? This one. Because on the other side, there is someone. Silly, I thought, but I bought the book. In a world of magic that I would like to believe in right now, maybe I felt you looking.

When we met, and merged, it was good. But I didn't know if you would want to come dancing with me. You said you like dancing. A lot of people do. But do you need it? Wouldn't work to have someone in the raving part of my life unless they need it too.

I started us off with a high tea, an afternoon dance party. Gay men and house music, basically. You met some of my people. There was a bit of a rift in the diagram at the time, so after each encounter I whispered whether they were Capulets or Montagues—with myself as Mercutia. I'd do a camp line read of "a plague on both your houses!" Which is either not funny, or too funny, in an actual plague.

We both got into the house music. The way you lost yourself in the dance—that seemed promising. But the floor was concrete. We didn't stay long. Home to fuck, in this bed, where now we also write.

The first time we went dancing together, to that high tea, I was more than a little nervous. There was so much light. There was COVID. What if I danced the wrong way at a rave and you didn't like me? But that was ludicrous. The point was to feel the music, to let myself in by letting go. What I thought, so clearly, on that dance floor was: shut the fuck up, you are dancing with a beautiful woman on a Sunday afternoon at the end of the world.

Next, we went to one of the smaller raves. It's a curious kind of date. You came to my place. I made dinner. We got high, fucked, got to sleep early. Woke to the alarm at four to be at the rave a half hour later. Dancing, not together, not as a couple, but close. Sensing these bodies, moving in sound, connected by sound.

You're into this. Lost in it. The default dance someone does at a rave, after a good hour or so, becomes so intimate. To rave one gives oneself over to this gestural body, arrayed among others. Your side-to-side step. That oscillation of the shoulder. How tender it makes me feel to be near you, lost too.

We're up the front. You are using the earplugs I got for J. Turns out they were a gift, a gesture toward ongoingness, just not the one I expected.

We caught a fair chunk of Mary Yuzovskaya's set, whose style I really like. I'm no expert on techno. The real heads would know better than me. I just like what I like. And I like these minimal, spacey tracks she selects.

We're vaping weed and dancing, feeling the sub-bass ripple through. You write fiction and I don't. Not exactly. You are not a character I can make up. I can only write what I feel and sense of you. You seem to be happy. Would you tell me if you weren't? Would I just feel it? I want to feel what you feel. I want to be here for your needs.

Yes, I was happy. You've got that right. I might not tell you if I wasn't. Not because I expect you to guess, but because I manage my emotions before I put them in front of anyone else. Or I like to believe I do.

Meanwhile over here, the xeno-euphoria is kicking in. After Mary, Pure Immanence play, which is my friend Nick and his DJ partner Kiddo. Flip into ravespace. It's all coming so easily. The flight into strange flesh, the strange flight out. Being here with you is helping me get out of myself. As Q would say, our being with others is best when it invites othering our being.

Dance until the flesh presses needs of its own. We take a break. Get water. Take a piss. Separate stalls. Check this face and hair in the mirror in the overlit bathroom while I wait for you.

These crip feet hurt, so rather than return to the dance, I take you by the hand to the back of the rave. I'm avoiding the spot where I was with J. A good spot, but that would be in poor taste. Anyway, it's you leading us now, elsewhere.

Perched on a plywood ledge, leaning together. Heat and sweat. I can taste you on me, mixed with my own taste, and I like it. Running a hand up your thigh. Into you. Feeling you flood over my fingers. Gasp. Enlustment. Feel like I'm offering to you, to the situation, all the states in which I'm free. Let our bodies be with each other when they're free.

What I also remember about that sex is that the beats were vibrating the plywood, and in turn vibrating my cunt, and that is also part of what made me cum. You and the music both fucked me.

We're there 'til the end. A little cluster of favorite ravers gather and chat before we all head home. There's N and A, E and Z, G and H. Sharing this state of being with each other after we all worked so hard. This labor of making nothing but each other in dance.

Back out of the rave continuum, into the cursed sun. An enormous flock of black birds crowd the roof of an apartment building on Bushwick Avenue. Having their own rave.

Back home to mine, and this bed, and sleep. When we wake, around eleven, you say that it's like we get an extra day into the weekend by getting up for a morning rave. It feels to me like you've found k-time. You're a raver now. Or always were.

Just to take it up a notch, next we go to the big Halloween rave. Office building in Manhattan. Three stories. The whole space a constructed situation. With light and fog, empty glass-walled office spaces become something else. A playground for nonlabor.

It's a fetish-wear party. You bought a black vinyl dress for it. Hot. I'm in some black mesh thing, suspenders, stockings and boots. Leftovers from my closet cross-dressing days.

Up on the third floor. We're stage left. Empty aluminum cans dancing on the bass bin right in front of me. They bounce to different heights, depending on how much liquid is left in them.

What I take to be three gay men in puppy masks gambol right next to us. Delightful. Less so the man in basic jeans and tee with his dick out. Half hard. He strokes it in a desultory way. Rubs it against another body. Looks consensual, sort-of. Hard to tell.[1]

I'm not paying much attention. What fills the senses is meat and heat—and strangeness. An idea seizes. As usual, this notion turns over for a while. Sixteen beats pass. Then it's decided: clambering on top of the bass bin. Facing the whole room, taking in the swaying and bobbing bodies, the energy, the heat, the sweat.

It's a little hard to dance up there as the top of the bin is narrow and it's vibrating like mad. I wonder for a moment if anyone recognizes me. Or if I'm making a fool of myself. Probably. And what's wrong with that? Lost to the xeno-euphoria of this othered body, bursting free of itself as itself.

Come back to check vitals. Thirst. You help me climb down. It'd be embarrassing to break a hip. We wander off into the labyrinth.[2] Find a quiet bar in a dark corner to get the water these mammal pod bodies both need. Wander downstairs to the ambient space. It's covered in low ottomans, covered in turn with a flounce of bodies, clad in black. Holding your hand so I don't lose you in the dark.

Don't see a space for us. So, back up to the third floor, but away from the dance floor, back into the maze. Threads of sound so we can find our way out. There's a glass-walled office bathed in red light with ropes for shibari but it seems we missed the show. Another fish-tank office lit in green. Two people sit cross-legged on the floor, staring into each other's eyes, hands entwined. We let them be.

By the elevator a man stands wedged into a corner. Head resting against the wall. Think of asking if he is ok but seems he just wants to cut the sensory overload for a bit, so I leave him. Eyes adjusting to the low light, it seems there's sofas strewn against the far wall. We find one in a quiet spot. Sit and chill. Hydrate. It's a no-photo party but I still take some discreet pictures of the ambience.

I have what you call "moves." *LOL you and your moves.* We're not alone here, but after thinking about it for thirty-two beats, still can't resist pulling one out of my bag of romantic and sexual tricks. This move, you know, from reading one of my other books: leaping into a straddle, onto your lap, tilting your chin up to kiss. Pressing this body into this other.

It's a move that's a question made of various touches. You touch back. It's pleasant, but there's a spear of sunlight coming in from somewhere. There can't be much longer in which to dance, and that's the immediate need. We're back on the floor. Until the beats stop.

Back in the summer of 2021, I'd broken up with a lover. Someone of whom I'm still fond in that lesbian way, that way of bringing treasured exes into your life. That ongoingness had to become something other than as lovers. After that, I'd gone a little crazy hooking up with other t-girls, including F and J. And then I found you.

Somewhere along the way, between late summer and the winter solstice, it was decided. You and I became an ongoing situation, with special rituals of joint being. Taking baths together. Talking through feelings. Writing together in bed. Going to raves. Dancing in secret caves of crystal time.

Morning raving became a particular ritual of ongoingness. SHYBOI closing out some warehouse space, brusque beats and brute light stalking the floor. Or Lychee, who I know a little from the Discord, animating a pocket rave, full of familiar bodies.[3]

Or that time we saw the promoter come over and whisper in the DJ's ear. Something was up. I only found out later from the Discord that someone had overdosed on GHB.[4] L called 911 but knew not to mention drugs, so only the ambulance would come, not the cops. L stayed with the fallen raver outside the venue, a little way down the street—actually practicing the codes of care that we all preach.

The DJ turned the volume down a notch and played an extra forty minutes so we would not all be out on the street—clogging it with car service, drawing attention—until the ambulance had come and gone. Not knowing any of that, we went home together happy and bone-tired. Back to this bed again.

Our favorite big party got pandemic relief money and went legit. Tickets for sale not just on discreet lists but to just anyone on Resident Advisor. Gave them the budget to book bigger DJs. One of their signature things is sound in the round: the DJ surrounded by dancers. Such a pleasure to watch DVS1 from behind, playing the CDJs, deft, sure, gentle as a talented lover might.[5]

Would have been a good morning except for the heavy police presence. There to remind us that our space becomes their space whenever they want and short of a riot there is nothing that we can do about it. The cops declared the party needed to end an hour early and came through at closing to clear us out. In the presence of so many filthy faggots, dykes, and trannies— for once they wore their masks. This is not the crowd to stage another Stonewall. The white language of queerness became a dialect of gentrification. Some of us have too much to lose.

That had always been a strictly no-photo party. Only this time someone made a TikTok on the dance floor. Last I looked it had 300,000 views. That party's inevitable overexposure will probably end one era of its ongoingness. Others will fill the niche.

You couldn't come to Takaaki Itoh, in that same little space where Lychee played.[6] Had to work your side hustle, as everyone does these days. I gave your ticket to one of the workers at Nowadays whom I know from both the Discord and Signal groups, who had kindly let me jump the queue a couple of times. Reparative discrimination.

A lot of punishers up the front when I got there at four. They seem to know each other. What I take to be a cis man fist pumps for five beats, then stands still. Then talks loudly to the cis woman beside him. I'm up against the speaker stack stage right. A great spot but they keep pushing me up against it. Think about it, then start making a traverse through the crowd to try stage left. One of them tries to stop me passing through like he owns the spot. A dick move.

Stage left has a cishet couple planted against the speakers. They're doing the rope-pull dance to each other, eyes locked, legs apart, arms grabbing air in front of the body, left then right. They don't flow with the people around them and are a bit aggressive about holding space, but I will come to admire the way they do this dance together. Four hours nonstop.

I'm between them and what I read as a lesbian couple rolling on molly. The smaller of the two has her back to me. The other, bigger one holds her tight, but being bigger, keeps pushing the little one onto me. I gently push back, smiling, and the big one apologizes. The little one is out of it and unaware of anything except her lover. Coupledom on the dance floor—the privatization of awareness. But I'm here for this dyke love.

Finally, the loud, annoying punisher crew starts to tire and leave the front line. Most cishet men can't let the beat fuck them. They can't even be switch with it to keep it going. They do their best to top the beat. They always cum too quick. They imagine they can outfuck the machine. That they're in charge. In the cockpit. They imagine they're the DJs of their own lives, and that the DJ is a figure of mastery, of commands. Silly boys.

I think of that scene in the movie *Barbarella*, where Duran Duran, concierge to the Great Tyrant of the alien city of Sogo, catches the earth woman Barbarella and puts her in his Excessive Machine.[7] He plays it like a DJ, extracting music from it and bodily pleasure from her. Delightful, only it doesn't stop. It keeps going. His desire is to kill her with technopleasure.

But he can't. She's Barbarella—Jane Fonda—and she outlasts him. Earth woman and alien machine cum together, burning up and burning out.

Duran Duran: "Wretched, wretched girl! What have you done to my Excessive Machine? You've undone it! You've undone me! Look! The energy cables are shrinking! You've turned them into faggots! You've blown out the Excessive Machine! You've blown all its fuses! Shame! Shame on you! You'll pay for this! Oh, I've got something in store for you! You'll wish you had died of pleasure before this day is done. Now you shall learn the wisdom of the lash! I'll do things to you that are beyond all known philosophies! Wait till I get my devices!"

I think of the city of Sogo from that movie as the rave continuum. I think of Duran Duran as the punisher, as the malign desire for control and mastery, over a technics that repeats and repeats itself, that can at best be pleasurably endured. The Excessive Machine will kill us all in the end. Some already know this.

I'm in ravespace, thoughts off wandering their own twisty city, while the body wraps itself into repetitive movement, to the sounds of the machines that Itoh coaxes rather than commands. I think about whether you'd like that movie or see it as ridiculous. *It's ridiculous.*

A and U show up, so I have some friendly and practiced bodies to be near. I'm on weed and mushrooms. I don't know what the name for that is. It's not a hippyflip or a candyflip. I'm going to call it a phylaflip: three kinds of life, each from a different phylum: basidiomycete (psilocybin), vascular (cannabis), and chordate (me). It's making each moment, each gesture, smear into the next, congealing time.

The way you describe being in these spaces and being on these dance floors is similar to the way I feel and the impressions these spaces and experiences have made on me. Which is why it really, really makes me want to dance. Makes me hungry for it. I do need it, and no matter how long we dance, when we're done, I want more.

I have a good view of Itoh on the decks. Looks like there's three minimal techno tracks playing on the three CDJs and he's tweaking how they play against each other. He's DJing in vertical and horizontal times. Worlds phase in and out of proximity to each other, refracting the angles of sideways time available so they fan out as spectra with different emotional color values.

There's a lot of fog and dim reddish light. Visual sense tamped down, kinesthetics ramped up.[8] It's a magical set. The build and release, gentle. It's a wander through wonders. There's a coolness to it, rooms for the dancers' own emotions to bloom and fruit. There's references back to certain sounds, maybe the nineties UK scene, but not too much.

Phylaflip can get heady. Now this letter to you is writing itself in my head while dancing. A little anxious about forgetting it, wondering if I should write it on my phone. This is a no-phone party—they even put a sticker over the camera—so I don't want to do that. I'm reconciled by the thought that I'll just write you a different letter, later.

Then I'm distracted by the thought that maybe what I'm experiencing here is a fourth aesthetic of dissociation. There's a certain sensibility in techno from which it departs. When the sounds fit neatly in the barest genre conventions but are lacking in any strong associations with past musics, while not relying either on those past associations that suggest a sonic future.

At once familiar, because conventional, and strange, but not disconcerting. How the surround sounds to itself.

This dissociation is something to do with time, historical time. Its concept hasn't come to me yet. I know what it isn't. It isn't hyperstition. It's not the future seeping into the present. There is no future at the moment. Nor is it hauntology. It's not a memorial for futures past.[9] We're in a sideways time, where time rambles and gets lost. It's a dissociated time, but not just as felt in this body. It is history itself as dysphoric, as unable to settle into its own body—metabolic rift.

Outside, where it's bright already, is some overlit, spectacular time. Hellbent on setting the world on fire. The Duran Durans of the world will play their Excessive Machines 'til they melt and burn—with us inside. In here, this situation, now that the punishers have left us, now that there's just us who feel this need—is a time we're dancing into being that's aside from the past that birthed us into this nightmare, and from father time waiting by to kill us all.

Delightfully tired and tits-out. Bra and top tied to the silver handbag. I take a break to recline on an old sofa, far from the dance floor. Z and L are here, and we chat about the show.

L is recovering from an injury. Dancing hard, he slipped in a puddle of his own sweat and put a shoulder out. A reset of the shoulder was performed onsite. Relying on each other, as far as we can. I ask Z what we'll do when everything ends, and we can't get our beats and 'mones anymore. Right away she says, "We're going down with the ship."

Now alone on the sofa. The blind over the front window had a tiny hole, through which a single beam of morning sunlight tropes through the mist and vapor, landing on my right breast.

That was last weekend. And then a new strain of virus. This weekend's raves get canceled, one by one. Both the Discord and Signal groups turn to collaboratively filtering information about COVID news and testing sites.[10] The rank order of disposability of our bodies is visible once again.

Frankie Decaiza Hutchinson: "Prior to this we had a certain barrier, even protection from the depths of depravity of the world, which guided us to imagine other, brighter futures. But our niche's intimate global fight can't help but feel naïve in the wake of this pandemic, like we've been buried in bass, unable to hear the greater noise."[11]

We stay in and phylaflip: Fuck, bathe, write, eat, repeat. Talk over feelings. About this ongoingness that we're making together. Dancing to the sweet unheard. This rhythm. What words can I say that I've not said to anyone before you? Could we have a kind of desire, of ongoingness, that is like a kind of techno? The kind without excessive language, overused. The kind without too much memory. The kind that dances.

Writing together in this bed. Taking breaks to be in our separate social media worlds. We don't follow each other and yet keep ending up in each other's feeds. It's uncanny. Diagrams aligning. You DM me from your Twitter feed.

Frog and Toad Bot: "Toad sipped his tea. 'Frog, he asked, are you making this up?' 'Maybe yes and maybe no,' said Frog." Your note underneath it reads: *You and your little autofiction*. Well yes, maybe I'm making it up here and there. But I'm not making up how I feel about you.

We're staying in bed for the day, writing. Cold out. Z and E in the next room, also hunkered down. Behind closed doors so we can pretend to have our own worlds. Z went out to get honey and I asked her to get milk too. "This is no land of milk and money," I quip, "but this is the apartment of milk and honey." Everyone laughs even though it's not funny.

The need. It's pressing. And not just on this transsexual body. *To exist inside those beats is like hacking into a new brain, one that doesn't hate my body, that can run on the DJ's track and not the track of my anxiety, that allows my body to be a fucking body.* Dancing will find its way to us.

Three-thirty in the morning. Wake with you wrapped around me. Untangle an arm, turn off the alarm. By a bit after four we're at the club, banging on a steel door seeping muffled beats. No answer. Bang on the door again. The bouncer, a large Black man, opens it, not for us but to throw some white guy out for having his camera out on the dance floor. "Doors closed at four," the bouncer declares. I'm smiling and holding out my vax pass and ID. He shrugs, checks our passes, and lets us in.

Nearly empty. There's maybe thirty people on the dance floor. Part of me wants to get in among them and feel their energy, but I hang back. I'm sensing where your body is and what our group decision is about this. You and I end up at the back, right in front of a speaker stack. There's good sound at the back so maybe we can "socially distance." It might be only a symbolic gesture as far as avoiding the viral vector goes but I'm sensing we feel better about it. *Sweetie, if you wanted to dance closer to the front, all you had to do was say so.*

The opening DJ got COVID, so Juliana Huxtable has been playing for six hours already with two or more to go. She's throwing down some heavy beats and a slew of her signature sounds. It's not the kind of techno I favor lately, but I love her talent. Jazz musicians improvise by pulling notes or chords out of a space of possibility into horizontal time. She pulls tracks out of a space of possibility in parallel vertical times—a kind of metajazz. Selecting the most unlikely-seeming sonic matches, this beat with that noise track with that snatch of vocal or melody. Sounds made free, up to the limits of what CDJs will do.

We are in our groove for three hours, taking turns to get water. Watching a few raver friends we know, and a bunch of strangers, up the front of the room. Every now and then the party monitor sitting to our right will get up and throw some spectacularly expansive moves across the almost empty floor.

Juliana flicks in some eighties postpunk tracks. I'm not loving these, being old enough to recall them. They're freighted with memory for me and maybe me alone in this younger crowd. You would at least have been born and alive when they were current. *Yes, I was born and alive for those songs and it did bother me a little to have memory thrown at me that way*. Still, I can ease back on the moves and admire how Juliana threads and layers those into others, jailbreaking eighties sounds from the tyranny of taste, shattering residual structures of feeling.

Then this body is moving again. I'm locked into some midrange series of sounds that come in and out of prominence, fading me in and out with it. Dissociating out of historical time. Only something in it sparks a memory. It's kin to a refrain from a familiar track, and for once I can place it. Almost.

It's either "Nannytown" or "Maroon" from the *Interstellar Fugitives* album, by Underground Resistance.[12] It's almost fitting that those track names on that album got switched at some point between the vinyl, the CD, and the streaming.

That track has a vocal, a stark male-sounding voice, but one beyond any singular being. Over the thud of a three-note bassline. They address the listener—me—in the second person. I've played that track so often that I know it, and hear it in my head, mixed over whatever Julianna is mixing.

This—is a voice from the past, they say. Standing in the future. Forever to haunt—me. I should never have done this to them. Because now they can never rest. They are: Black, electric. Strong electric. That's the negative, unvoiced noise of techno.[13] The blackness of techno itself. This past haunts the present, unburied, restless, electric. This future will forever ghost any party that can't dance to the noise with which it surrounds.

Nanny Town was a Maroon village in the Blue Mountains of Jamaica, home of a resistance led for a time by an Ashanti woman from what is now Ghana, known as Queen Nanny. I know this because I just looked it up on my machine, here in bed with you. But what does that other history, of Black Marronage and resistance, have to do with techno?[14]

Truth is, my white ass is haunted by that voice, from that track. Surrounded by a past that is not a lost future but a past that prevents there ever being one. That clutches at our fleeting moments of ongoingness with a cold hand. That past in which the slave was a thing, a machine. That past in which the slave as a machine was the prototype of the machine as slave.[15]

They're not here tonight, but I think back to last weekend and those cishet men who don't want to be sonically fucked by techno. I think of it in part as the straight cis man's horror of being penetrable, of being fuckable.[16] A state he associates with powerlessness. That which is technical can only be that which he masters. For him it's not what you give yourself over to, not that which you seduce.

His master's voice. He can think of the world only through his mastery of it. And in treating what surrounds him as the object of his gaze and of his mastery, he also comes to be anxious that it will sneak up on him unseen, envelop him, take him in. For him, the surround is a space of anxiety, the darkness beyond what he can see, from which he hears strange and disturbing sounds.

Perhaps there's other residues of white panic. Fear of the surround, of darkness, of sounds that could be human, or alien, or animal, or machines—fear of blackness. The restless reminder of that which is enslaved, that which is treated as an object, commodity, fungible as value and as flesh, yet as having a need of its own, the need to get free, to get lost. And then the white panic that in doing so it will want revenge.

Techno, not as genre but as technique, lets digital machines speak. Not unlike the way jazz lets analog instruments speak. Sounds at the limit of what the machine or the instrument can do to get free. Blackness in sound as the technique of making the thing free to sound off as itself and to take the human with it, into movement, into feeling, into sensation.

Feels like that's what we're all doing here, while Julianna plays, when I dance, when we dance, or when we are in bed together, working on our laptops. We try to play along, inside the Excessive Machine, with no fantasy that we could ever dominate it. Try instead to make at least a part of it that a part of the human can live with.

Is that a black need? I don't know. Is that a trans need? I

feel that. To turn some small part of a technics made against us or without us to our wants. I take a break from dancing to get water. I run into G. Ask how they're feeling about tonight. "Apocalypse Prom vibes," they say, and I laugh. They compliment me on my skirt and ask where it's from. Have to admit I got it on online, from Dolls Kill. A brand called Current Mood. Black with the word OFFLINE in white, in English and Japanese katakana. Sometimes the best thing about raves is they get us offline for hours.

It's light out now. Outside, the spectacle reigns. A disintegrating spectacle, we can all see it on our cracked little screens. In here, the screen at least is pushed aside. It's still spectacle, but it's what's at its edges, what surrounds the image, the eyeless ambient noise.[17] A good rave is still spectacle, but reduced to its minimal, formal elements: beats and fog and diffracted light. Our devotion to it almost religious. A religion without content, a faith of pure media form.[18]

What was once outside the spectacle, the two forces that might disrupt it: pollution and the proletariat.[19] But we lost. Now only pollution surrounds it as its externality, the remnant of historical time. Of all the liberation movements only one succeeded without limit: the Carbon Liberation Front. It freed an element from earthbound life, floating free, making an enemy of our old comrade the sun.

Dysphoric planet; metabolic rift.[20] History won't come to the rescue. With our defeat, there are now only two official parties: the one that wants to kill us and the one that will let us die. This was not how the story was supposed to go. Now it seems we take refuge in the rave, a fragment of spectacle, reduced to an almost contentless form, refuge from history.

And so, finally: the fourth kind of dissociation: world-historical. To be absent from scarifying history from eleven at night 'til eight in the morning, to hold dear this other time, and each other. For 75,600 beats, between which are infinitesimal pores of sideways time.

Feeling the kick drum sound, clean and clear. Let's name this world-historical dissociation after the technique that makes that sound: *sidechain time*. I once asked Z, who is a technical girl, to explain sidechaining to me. "It's when you use a sound, such as a kick drum, as the signal to compress the loudness of other sounds in the mix when the kick drum kicks, so it booms in a sonic clearing."

Each rave in the rave continuum sidechains a signal that k-time can happen, clean and clear, the noise of historical time compressed down toward silence, but just for the moment that the rave kicks against the pricks. The rave continuum happens, and feels like a steady techno beat, only because each rave sidechains all other time. An ongoingness possible—for now—only because it silences all that which will end it. Not much, perhaps, but it keeps some of us in animated life.

There is merit in sharing the pessimism. Everyone is experiencing it. Helps us all feel our way through it. A commiseration. An articulation. It makes it okay not to pretend that some big hope is going to save us. It's about how a person saves herself, inside of this darkness, at the end of the world, by finding some way to exist within it.

Once you and I get back home to my little room, we're quickly asleep. I wake up before you, laced into your limbs. It's warm and dark in the apartment of milk and honey. There's another fragment of a vocal, by the eighties Brit-pop diva Sade in my head. Did I dream her or was she in Julianna's set? Gently extracting a hand, I text Julianna. She's still up, and texts right back: "Yes from set! I played 'Cherish the Day,' a footwork remix." The fragment, on loop, soundtrack in my head to holding you.

1–3   On Q's rooftop during the COVID pandemic lockdown. She was teaching herself to DJ. A played too, plus a few other DJs. B, E, H, P, T. V and Z came through. N had access to the gear for free as there was nobody to rent it.

4   Lockdown-era street raves. This is the Regression one, at The Hole. Early, before it really got cute. Shot from the railway overpass.

5–6   The railyards by Newtown Creek, after we lost G and the others. E, Z, and I didn't want to be in the middle of this, so we worked around its edges. Shortly after this, the drunk girl landed on us.

7   Post-lockdown. Rave ethnographer at work, sitting it out to make some notes on my phone. In those boots.

8   After I lost it and had to do breathing exercises up on the sofa by the darkroom. I have a less fuzzy shot too, but this one is the mood.

9   The better raves have a no-photo rule, at least on the dance floor. It's an almost religious injunction. This is a regular putting his

hand over my camera as I try to photograph the lights on the ceiling. He was right. I was too close to the dancers.

10   I want to honor the no-photo rule when there is one. To not interrupt the energy of the dancers. I also want to document ambiences. To push the limits of what the iPhone 12 can do. Its algorithms are designed to search for faces or shapes or landscapes. I want to picture instead things like light refracting off fog.

11   Rave bag—an important and very personal piece of kit for most ravers. madison moore calls hers Sheila. I don't have a name for mine. Slung on it at the left, a wrap to warm me against the cool night air on the walk home. On the right, the cylinder containing my earplugs. Inside: iPhone 12, cash, credit card, ID, vape, fan, and a very tiny book to read if I get bored—selections from Candy Darling's diaries.

12   Jasmine and Anya playing b2b at my sixtieth birthday, Bossa Nova Civic Club, September 8, 2021. Far left is cranberry thunderfunk, who stepped in to do the lighting.

13   DJ Syanide playing Dweller Festival #1, Bossa Nova Civic Club, February 8, 2020.

14   Nick Bazzano, playing with Kiddo as Pure Immanence, 2022. Taken right at the end of the party.

15   January Hunt playing Funneled Smoke, October 4, 2019.

16   Cheating with my own boundaries about photographing ambiences, but I just wanted to remember these two ravers kissing, as the early morning light streams in from the chill-out yard. Enlustment.

17   Lighting design by Kip Davis for a Halloween rave on three floors of an empty Manhattan office building.

18   Light refracted through fog and steam. How ravespace might feel if one could picture it.

19 How xeno-euphoria feels, when one can't stand still.

20 Bossa Nova Civic Club on a very quiet morning.

21 That maze of a venue. I'm not the only one to get lost there.

22 The shibari rope, hanging in a vacant office building in Manhattan. Part of a beautifully crafted situation. The office repurposed for labors of pure expenditure.

23 Bossa Nova Civic Club on my sixtieth birthday, September 8, 2021.

24 After it's over. When I looked at the image later, I saw that someone had forgotten their little rave bag on the table.

25 With E and Z on the way home.

26 Bushwick in the background, mixer in front. A small gathering on a railway overpass, a little weekend situation.

Many of these concepts I've sampled and modified from others.

concept A good fact is mostly true about something in particular; a good *concept* is slightly true about a lot of things. A fact is a note; a concept is a chord. Sometimes they make soundings, as *resonant abstractions*.

constructed situation A situation is where agency meets concrete forms that shape its expression. A *constructed situation* brings a certain art and intention to give form to how agency might express its willfulness, its need. The specific ambience the rave as a constructed situation aims to make is *k-time*.

coworker A social type labeled by ravers to denote a kind of nonraver. For coworkers, a rave is a leisure activity outside of work time. Likely to be overly enthusiastic. Will be telling coworkers stories about it Monday morning. The coworker does not feel the need to merge into *k-time* to engage the dissociated aesthetic states it enables.

enlustment One of several dissociative aesthetics that might be found in *k-time*. To feel body as an intense kernel of expansive lust indifferent to *ongoingness*. A different need from *ravespace* in that it's a dissociation out of subjectivity but into flesh. Different also from *xeno-euphoria* in that it doesn't commune with strangeness but with the most ordinarily mammalian. These are maybe all states of "ressociation" if one were to further develop these practices toward their concept.

femmunism A collective state emerging out of a *constructed situation* from which masculinity that expresses itself as domination is subtracted as technically obsolete. Achieved in part by *reparative discrimination*. It has no necessary *ongoingness*, no memory, no relation to desired futures, and appears only momentarily. Where girls and their familiars get their rave on, where *ravespace*, *enlustment*, and *xeno-euphoria* can happen among them. Not utopian as it can still all go wrong. It touches the *surround*.

junkspace Urban ambiences that hover between decaying forms of usage and novel potentials. Where a city's tendencies of coherent spatial organization fail. Good locations for *constructed situations* but inevitably prey to *style extraction*.

k-time What the *constructed situation* of a rave aims to generate. *K-time* is machine time amplified to the moment where it splits from duration and takes the body sideways, possibly into *enlustment*, *ravespace*, *xeno-euphoria*, or other as yet unnamed aesthetics—all without memory or expectations. A dissociative time, a ketamine time. Moments of k-time appear to blend into the *rave continuum*.

ongoingness The time of desire, of history, felt nowadays as the scar of impossible futures, whereas *enlustment, xeno-euphoria*, and *ravespace* inhabit *k-time*, a time sprung out sideways within the *constructed situation*. Rather than practices of *ongoingness*, *k-time* coaxes ravers into finite, detached sideways times, free from the theology of "happily ever after."

punisher A social type labeled by ravers to denote, firstly, a kind of non-raver. Often, but not always, straight, white, cis men. Treats the space as a spectacle for their entertainment, contributes nothing, gets in the way. An even more unpleasant kind of *punisher* is internal to the scene, its self-appointed police. That from which *femmunism* withdraws, seeking refuge in the *surround*.

rave continuum Every good rave that has ever happened or will ever happen makes contact with the continuum, which is a time that exists outside of every other time. The continuum folds moments of *k-time* together so that their tracks mix. *Ravers* feel it as continuous time, and who's to say it isn't? The rave continuum can open into *sidechain time*, which mutes historical time like a series of kick-drum beats, so that raves sound into the *surround*, through the chatter.

raver A self-identified social type. Those who really need to rave. Who seek out *k-time*, who need *ravespace*, *enlustment*, and/or *xeno-euphoria*. Or perhaps some other states I have yet to observe, or as yet unknown to anyone. The raver overlaps with, but is also other to, the *punisher*, the *coworker*, or to various other social types: the club kid, the burner, the circuit gay, and so on.

ravespace One of at least three needs that drive *ravers* to the rave as *constructed situation*. When *k-time* spools out—that's where *ravespace* can be sought. Dissociation into existing within and without the body simultaneously, free of selfhood. Different from *enlustment*, dissociation from self into body, and *xeno-euphoria*, dissociation out of self into flesh-otherness.

reparative discrimination Entry through the threshold to *constructed situations* selectively granted to those who need it most, so that some parcel of *femmunism* may be bestowed for a moment, that the *surround* may be touched, before *style extraction* takes it away.

resonant abstractions Throw the body into situations that generate sensations, parsed as perceptions, gathered as *concepts*, which work like impersonal characters in the autotheory text. All of the *concepts* in this glossary are such.

sidechain time The time of collective, world-historical dissociation. Each rave in the *rave continuum* sidechains a *k-time* signal, clean and clear, through the noise of historical time, which it compresses down toward silence, but just for the moment of rave. The rave continuum happens, and feels like a steady techno beat, only because each rave sidechains all other time, that the rave might spool sideways into the *surround*.

style extraction The commodification of gestures generated in *constructed situations*. It is an industrial procedure that makes *junkspace* valuable real estate. *Reparative discrimination* is an only partial and temporary remedy for those whose style is being extracted, as it makes *femmunism* possible, but maybe only in *k-time*.

surround That refuge beyond what can be surveilled, disciplined, and contained, whose being is blackness. Which *femmunism* might touch, with which it might mingle, when invited.

xeno-euphoria Forms of bodily wellness achievable only through external agents, which at the same time produce euphoric states of welcome strangeness. An alternate, but not incompatible, need to *ravespace* or *enlustment* that can be derived from *constructed situations* that generate *k-time*.

1. Rave as Practice

1   On the rise and fall of the ecstasy-era raves, see Silcott, *Rave America*; Collin, *Altered State*; Reynolds, *Energy Flash*; and Collin, *Rave On*. Holman and Zawadzki, *Parties for the People*, has thoughtful documentation and recollection of a particular Northern English scene. There won't be a literature review as this is not that kind of book. Think of these end notes as that. Or as potential reading lists. Or as snapshots of my room at various stages in this work, with books and photocopies in piles around and even in the bed where I often work.

2   On urban subcultures and music, see Hebdige, *Subculture*; Chambers, *Urban Rhythms*; McKay, *Senseless Acts of Beauty*; Gilbert and Pearson, *Discographies*; St. John, *Technomad*; and Thornton, *Club Cultures*.

3   For me, the classic on participant observation is still Becker, *Outsiders*. See also Esther Newton's pioneering queer ethnography, *Mother Camp*. I always learn from my New School colleague Terry Williams. See his *Soft City*, although his and his students'

encounters with trans nightlife might say more about cis people than us.

4 In terms of an operative sketch for a method, I've learned a lot from Ahmed, *Queer Phenomenology*; and Salamon, *Assuming a Body*. I'm influenced by Gayle Salamon's reading of Maurice Merleau-Ponty's phenomenology of the body, but in this book, I'm looking for limit cases, particularly of transsexual embodiment, raver embodiment, that might exceed these concepts.

5 For me, autofiction is a form of writing for those whom the bourgeois novel could accommodate only in the margins: those not straight, not white, not men, not cis. Those who can't hide behind the alibi of fiction as if their kind could be said to already exist, who have to write their world into existence through their own name. For instance, see Genet, *Our Lady of the Flowers*; Dustan, *Works of Guillaume Dustan*, vol. 1; and Lorde, *Zami*.

6 See Fournier, *Autotheory*. As with autofiction, there are a lot of possible genealogies for autotheory. I happen to like this feminist one. To which I'd add the early writing of Susan Stryker, such as "Dungeon Intimacies" and "LA by Night," and Paul Preciado's *Testo Junkie*.

7 In *Energy Flash*, Simon Reynolds thinks the use in London of the term *rave* for all-night parties may have West Indian roots. See Steve McQueen's *Lover's Rock*, a lovingly rendered film set mostly at a West Indian house party in London.

8 On queer uses of dance music, see Adayemi et al., *Queer Nightlife*; Geffen, *Glitter Up*; Lawrence, *Love Saves the Day*; Lawrence, *Life and Death*; Salkind, *Do You Remember House?*; Buckland, *Impossible Dance*; and Garcia, "Alternate History of Sexuality."

9 Brown Jr., *Assembling a Black Counter-culture*. This and most other block quotes, dropped in like samples, are edited and condensed. For DeForrest, techno is a specifically African American music, one of a series of forms that evolve out of the experience

of slavery. Others follow Paul Gilroy in placing Black musical cultures in a diasporic perspective. See Gilroy, *Darker than Blue*. On blackness and dance music, see also Miller, *Rhythm Science*; Tate, *Flyboy 2*; Eshun, *More Brilliant than the Sun*; Brar, *Teklife*; Goodman, *Sonic Warfare*; and Muggs, *Bass, Mids, Tops*.

10 Treating dissociation as aesthetic rather than pathological is a practice I've had help with from other trans writers. See Wallenhorst, "Like a Real Veil"; and Markbreiter, "Cruel Poptimism."

11 On disability and raves, see Beery, "Crip Rave."

12 Harney and Moten, *Undercommons*, 19. The undercommons is the best-known concept (if it is a concept) from that text, but I want to explore the surround instead. See also Moten, *In the Break*.

13 Harney and Moten, *Undercommons*, 50

14 On blackness, trans-ness, and sound, see Weheliye, *Phonographies* (where trans-ness is not all that well handled). On blackness and trans-ness, see Snorton, *Black on Both Sides*; Gossett, Stanley, and Burton, *Trap Door*; Bey, *Black Trans Feminism*; Stanley, *Atmospheres of Violence*; Stallings, *Funk the Erotic*; Moore, *Fabulous*; and von Reinhold, *LOTE*.

15 Sadler, *Situationist City*; Koolhaas et al., *Constant*; and Prestsaeter, *These Are Situationist Times!*

16 Situationist practices (perhaps more than theories) found their way into anarchist-inspired free rave movements. See, for example, Harrison, *Dreaming in Yellow.*

17 Morgan Page, @morganmpage, on Twitter, February 14, 2020.

18 Gornick, *Situation and Story*.

2. Xeno-euphoria

1 On thresholds and the in-between, see Eyck, *Child*.

2 The dolls, in their own words: Lady Chablis, *Hiding My Candy*;

Daelyn and Watson, *My Life Is No Accident*; Duff and Lake, *Unsinkable Bambi Lake*; Newman, *I Rise*; Huxtable, *Mucus in My Pineal Gland*; and Barton, *Summer I Got Bit*. Spanish-speaking version: Ojeda, *Never, Ever Coming Down*; Gentili, *Faltas*. Ballroom is another adjacent world, but again those are not my stories to tell. See Tucker, *And the Category Is . . .*

3 See Diana Goetsch's *This Body I Wore* on her experiences as straight people's walk on the wild side in New York nightlife.

4 Quotes from Nick Bazzano are from a meeting we had for a thing we were planning to do together for the "Acid Communism" conference at the Haus der Kulturen der Welt in Berlin. The idea was that the conference would give us an excuse to hit the Berlin clubs. The pandemic put an end to that plan, and I did the event via Zoom by myself.

5 Koolhaas, "Junkspace"; Jameson, "Future City."

6 Muñoz, *Cruising Utopia*. In raving I might be looking for a trans time that is not a queer time. See also Edelman, *No Future*; Halberstam, *In a Queer Time and Place*; Allen, *There's a Disco Ball Between Us*.

7 Puar, "I Would Rather Be a Cyborg."

8 On the Berlin scene in the nineties, see Denk and von Thülen, *Klang der Familie*; and Goetz, *RAVE*. On Berlin's sonic scenes, see Hanford, *Coming to Berlin*.

9 On the Sydney queer nightlife scene, see Fiona McGregor's novel *Chemical Palace* and her nonfiction work *Buried, Not Dead*.

10 Walker, "Mounting."

11 Heartscape, *Psycho Nymph Exile*, 64–65.

12 Jessica Dunn Rovinelli, personal communication, June 18, 2022. See Rovinelli, *So Pretty*.

13 On expenditure, see Bataille, *Accursed Share*. The "new narrative" writers took Bataille in a queer direction. See Boone, *Dismembered*; and Glück, *Jack the Modernist*, especially the sex

club scene. I must also acknowledge the influence for me here of Trieu, *Future Subject Matter*.

3. Ketamine Femmunism

1   On rave culture during the lockdown, see van der Heide, *Techno/ Globalization/Pandemic*. On New York during the lockdown, see Moss, *Feral City*.

2   On the effects of the start of the AIDS pandemic on New York queer life, see Schulman, *The Gentrification of the Mind*. And on developing concepts for a pandemic, see Treichler, *How to Have a Theory*.

3   Zaveri, "Rave under the Kosciuszko Bridge"; Colyar, "New York Nightlife Never Stopped"; Lipsky, "How the Illegal Rave Scene Thrives"; Witt, "Clubbing Is a Lifeline."

4   Unpublished text read by Hannah at the East River Park Amphitheater, August 11, 2021, where I ran into R. See also Baer, "Dance until the World Ends."

5   For a more comedic account of this side of queer and trans Brooklyn life, see Fitzpatrick, *The Call Out*.

6   Rose, "Janny's Delivery Service." See also Spade, *Mutual Aid*.

7   Given the situation, a tactical revision of Hall's "socialism without guarantees." Hall, *Hard Road to Renewal*, 183.

8   On the brightly colored plastic bags of fruit-flavored alcohol that New Yorkers call nutcrackers, see Herbert, "On the Trail."

9   Fulton, "Jasmine Infiniti."

10 See Eichhorn, *Adjusted Margin*, on how xerography changed the look of urban space and enabled an earlier iteration of queer urban life.

11 Kleist, "On the Marionette Theater."

12 Goetz, *RAVE*, 78. Can't help thinking he would have been such a punisher at raves—especially to women.

13 Met a girl in Berlin after my book launch. We got talking, and this idea popped out of the conversation. I think her name was Benjamin. Thanks, babe.

14 Plant, *Writing on Drugs*. On trans writing on drugs, see Baer, *Trans Girl Suicide Museum*; Wark, *Reverse Cowgirl*.

15 On this era without desire or history, see Azuma, *Otaku*. The raver is a more embodied, (sometimes) less masculine, less reclusive inversion of the otaku as social type, maybe.

16 Fisher, "Acid Communism," in Fisher, *K-Punk*, 751–70. Jeremy Gilbert says that some of his work and ideas ended up in that draft document. See Gilbert, "Psychedelic Socialism."

17 Vitos, "Along the Lines of the Roland TB-303."

18 See Niermann and Simon, *Solution 275–294*; Adamczak, *Yesterday's Tomorrow*; Otolith Group, *Long Time between Suns*.

19 Preciado, *Counter-sexual Manifesto*; Plant, *Zeroes and Ones*.

20 Fisher, "Exiting the Vampire's Castle," in Fisher, *K-Punk*, 437–46. I feel Mark's pain in that essay. I've reframed it by grouping together the punishers who act out and the ones that call out.

4. Enlustment

1 Gabriel, *Kissing Other People*, 82. The dream poems in this book are the collective psychogeographic *rêve* of a Brooklyn diagram not too far removed from the one of this book.

2 On house music, see Salkind, *Do You Remember House?*; Bidder, *Pump Up the Volume*; Cowley, *Mechanical Fantasy Box*; and for a tantalizing glimpse of the transsexual house music scene in New York, see Thaemlitz, *Nuisance*.

3 Adorno, *Culture Industry*, 46–47.

4 moore, "Hacking into the Now," 9.

5 Sandy Stone, in a Facebook comment, date unknown.

6 thunderfunk, *outer][space*, 28. Much indebted to Tim for his book, occasional conversations, the Discord he runs, and for being such a great raver to dance next to.

7 Serrano, *Whipping Girl*.

8 Dean, *Blog Theory*. This text can be read as responding to her on mediation and the decline of symbolic efficiency.

9 Ngai, *Our Aesthetic Categories*.

10 Burial, featuring The Space Ape, "Space Ape."

11 With apologies to Walter Benjamin. This is may be what writing was for Kathy Acker; see Acker, *Bodies of Work*.

5. Resonant Abstraction

1 On methods of rave ethnography, see O'Grady, "Interrupting Flow."

2 On percepts, affects, and concepts, see Deleuze and Guattari, *What Is Philosophy?*

3 For something like autofiction with a trans sensibility, see Fleishmann, *Time Is the Thing*; Sycamore, *Freezer Door*; Huxtable, *Mucus in My Pineal Gland*; Stryker, "LA by Night"; and Stryker, "Dungeon Intimacies."

4 Asger Jorn and Noël Arnaud's *La Langue Verte* was the inspiration here. A parody of the structural anthropology of Levi-Strauss, it contains "kinship diagrams" for Latin Quarter bohemians, in which basically everyone fucks everyone.

5 On the complexities of noncarceral queer community justice, see Schulman, *Conflict Is Not Abuse*; Thom, *I Hope We Choose Love*; and Heartscape, "Hot Allostatic Load."

6 On socializing in the age of social media extraction, see Nakamura, *Digitizing Race*; Lovink, *Social Media Abyss*; and Chun, *Discriminating Data*.

7   On New York psychogeography, see Solnit and Jelly-Schapiro, *Nonstop Metropolis*.

8   Quoted in Stosuy, "On Connecting Your Work."

9   For some versions of Brooklyn white trans-girl life, see Binne, *Nevada*; and Peters, *Detransition, Baby*. See also the as-yet-uncollected writings of the late Bryn Kelly, and the podcast by Macy Rodman and Theda Hammel, *Nymphowars*.

10 Bergsonist and Speaker Music, *Sublime Language of My Century*.

11 See van Veen, "Technics."

12 On "social types" and urban interactions in urban landscapes of commodified leisure, see Clark, *Painting of Modern Life*; and Benjamin, *Charles Baudelaire*.

13 Condensed from Rodman, "Berlin."

14 See this autofictional account of the life of a Brooklyn style-extractor: Segal, *Mercury Retrograde*.

15 On being the older raver, see O'Grady and Madill, "Being and Performing 'Older' Woman"; Bentley, "Have Things Really Changed?"; and Bell, "Really Techno."

16 See Alabanza, *Overflow*, a one-woman play set in a club toilet. It's a straight club in London, so the toilets are segregated, whereas at queer New York raves they're not.

17 Huxtable, *Mucus in My Pineal Gland*, 91.

18 One could think of the psychogeography of Brooklyn nightlife comparatively as well as historically. See, for instance, Hossfeld Etyang, Nyairo, and Sievers, *Ten Cities*; Cokes et al., *You Got to Get In*; Saldanha, *Psychedelic White*; and Kontra, *Location TBA*.

19 A point many insisted on at the "Nightlife Townhall" held at Nowadays, organized by Miss Parker and T. T. Britt, accessed January 21, 2021, https://soundcloud.com/djmissparker/nowadays-nightlife-townhall-audio.

20 Moskowitz, *How to Kill a City*, 183–84. On New York gentrification, see also Moss, *Vanishing New York*. On urban extraction, see also Pasquinelli, *Animal Spirits*.

21 Raunig, *Dividuum*.

22 Mak, "In Arcadia Ego."

23 For a brief tour of (Western) nightlife photography where one might find queer and trans people, see Brassaï, *Paris by Night*; van der Elsken, *Love on the Left Bank*; Strömholm, *Les Amies de Place Blanche*; Goldin, *Other Side*; Rivera, *Provisional Notes*; Bratton, *Bound by Night*; and the zine *Real Cool Time*, produced by J. Jackie Baier from 2014 to 2019, some of which can be seen at http://fotografie.jackiebaier.de.

24 There's an essay to be written on queer theory's bad takes on *Paris Is Burning* and ballroom in general. On ballroom, see instead Tucker, *And the Category Is . . .* On blackness, Black feminism, Black queerness, and Black sonic aesthetics, besides Weheliye, *Phonographies*, I have learned a lot from Brooks, *Liner Notes for the Revolution*; Campt, *Listening to Images*; Duplan, *Blackspace*; Nyong'o, *Afro-Fabulations*; and Russell, *Glitch Feminism*.

25 Moore, "DARK ROOM."

26 Davis, *Plastic Matter*.

27 Russom, "Hostile to Categorization," 115.

28 See Sicko, *Techno Rebels*. On the political economic context of Detroit, let's not forget its history of revolutionary labor struggles, see Georgiakis and Surkin, *Detroit*.

6. Excessive Machine

1 Probably not. We saw the same man at a later iteration of that rave, rubbing himself against dancers. Had a jacket over his arm, possibly to hide that his dick was out. He rubbed against me. Then did it again. So I smacked him in the face. He took that as

an opportunity to get in my face and tell me I am a "bad person," while pressing his whole body against me. You grabbed my hand and led me out of the dance floor. He followed us for a bit then gave up. I told a friend who was working the party about him, but he was nowhere to be seen by then.

2 I'm taken by this version of the Minotaur and the labyrinth story that sees it as a memory of the provincial Greek awe at the Minoan metropolis: Nicolai and Wenzel, *Four Times through the Labyrinth*.

3 This is a recording of that set: Lychee, *Sunrise at Locked Groove*.

4 Some raves are fine with the use of other drugs but not that one, which is controversial. See Blanchard, "Banning GHB."

5 On the history and art of the DJ, see Brewster and Broughton, *Last Night*.

6 This is a recording of that set: Itoh, *Locked Groove Transmission #02*.

7 Vadim, *Barbarella*. The character's name is in the credits as Durand Durand, but I prefer the other spelling, as used by the eighties new romantic pop band.

8 I learned a lot from the way the late Randy Martin thought of kinesthetics as postcapitalist allegory. See Martin, *Knowledge LTD*.

9 On hyperstitition, see Eshun, *More Brilliant than the Sun*. On hauntology, see Fisher, "Metaphysics of Crackle."

10 "Collaborative filtering" is a term used by Geert Lovink to describe the collective labor of using social media to generate useful concepts and information. See Lovink, *My First Recession*.

11 Hutchinson, "Club Activism," 53

12 Underground Resistance, *Interstellar Fugitives*.

13 Isham, "Noise Is the Nigga of Sounds."

14 Robinson, *Black Marxism*.

15   Chude-Sokai, *Sound of Culture*.

16   Theweleit, *Male Fantasies*; Hocquenghem, *Homosexual Desire*.

17   On the edges of the screen, see Galloway, *Interface Effect*.

18   I offered a different language for something like this in Galloway, Thacker, and Wark, *Excommunication*.

19   Debord, *Sick Planet*.

20   Rosenberg, "Afterword."

Acker, Kathy. *Bodies of Work*. London: Serpent's Tail, 2006.

Adamczak, Binni. *Yesterday's Tomorrow: On the Loneliness of Communist Specters and the Reconstruction of the Future*. Translated by Adrian Nathan West. Cambridge, MA: MIT Press, 2021.

Adayemi, Kemi, Kareem Khubchandani, and Ramón H. Rivera-Servera, eds. *Queer Nightlife*. Ann Arbor: University of Michigan Press, 2021.

Adorno, Theodor. *The Culture Industry: Selected Essays on Mass Culture*. Edited by Jay Bernstein. London: Routledge, 1991.

Ahmed, Sarah. *Queer Phenomenology: Orientations, Objects, Others*. Durham, NC: Duke University Press, 2006.

Alabanza, Travis. *Overflow*. London: Bush Theatre and Methuen Drama, 2021.

Allen, Jafari. *There's a Disco Ball Between Us: A Theory of Black Gay Life*. Durham, NC: Duke University Press, 2022.

Azuma, Hiroki. *Otaku: Japan's Database Animals*. Minneapolis: University of Minnesota Press, 2009.

Baer, Hannah. "Dance until the World Ends." *Artforum*, December 2021. https://www.artforum.com/print/202110/hannah-baer-on-rave -and-revolution-87233.

Baer, Hannah. *Trans Girl Suicide Museum*. Los Angeles: Hesse, 2019.

Baier, J. Jackie. *Real Cool Time*. Berlin: self-published, 2014–2019.

Barton, Joss. *The Summer I Got Bit*. St. Louis: self-published, 2020.

Bataille, Georges. *The Accursed Share*. Minneapolis: University of Minnesota Press, 1984.

Becker, Howard. *Outsiders: Studies in the Sociology of Deviance*. New York: Free Press, 1997.

Beery, Zoë. "Crip Rave Is the Revolutionary Collective Prioritizing Accessibility." *Resident Advisor*, May 26, 2022. https://ra.co/features/4000.

Bell, Julia. "Really Techno." *White Review*, June 2018. https://www.thewhitereview.org/feature/really-techno/.

Benjamin, Walter. *Charles Baudelaire: A Lyric Poet in the Era of High Capitalism*. Translated by Harry Zohn. London: Verso, 1997.

Bentley, Donna Cynthia. "Have Things Really Changed or Is It Just Me? Ageing and Dance Music Culture." *Dancecult* 11, no. 1 (2019): 97–100.

Bergsonist and Speaker Music. *The Sublime Language of My Century*. New York: bizaarbizaar, 2020.

Bey, Marquis. *Black Trans Feminism*. Durham, NC: Duke University Press, 2022.

Bidder, Sean. *Pump Up the Volume: A History of House Music*. London: Macmillan, 2001.

Binne, Imogen. *Nevada*. New York: Topside, 2013.

Blanchard, Sessi Kuwabara. "Banning GHB at Raves Is Dangerous." *Filter*, February 11, 2020, https://filtermag.org/ghb-ban-raves/.

Boone, Bruce. *Dismembered: Selected Poems, Stories, and Essays*. Callicoon, NY: Nightboat Books, 2020.

Brar, Dhanveer Singh. *Teklife/Ghettoville/Eski: The Sonic Ecologies of Black Music in the Twenty-First Century*. London: Goldsmiths, 2021.

Brassaï. *Paris by Night*. Paris: Flammarion, 2012.

Bratton, Elegance. *Bound by Night*. Portland, OR: Wild Life, 2014.

Brewster, Bill, and Frank Broughton. *Last Night a DJ Saved My Life: The History of the Disc Jockey*. New York: Grove, 2000.

Brooks, Daphne. *Liner Notes for the Revolution: The Intellectual Life of Black Feminist Sound*. Cambridge, MA: Belknap, 2021.

Brown, DeForrest, Jr. *Assembling a Black Counter-culture*. New York: Primary Information, 2022.

Buckland, Fiona. *Impossible Dance: Club Culture and Queer World-Making*. Middletown, CT: Wesleyan University Press, 2002.

Burial, featuring The Space Ape. "Space Ape." London: Hyperdub Records, 2014. https://hyperdub.bandcamp.com/track/burial-spaceape.

Campt, Tina. *Listening to Images*. Durham, NC: Duke University Press, 2017.

Chambers, Iain. *Urban Rhythms: Pop Music and Popular Culture*. New York: St. Martin's, 1985.

Chude-Sokai, Louis. *The Sound of Culture: Diaspora and Black Techno-poetics*. Middletown, CT: Wesleyan University Press, 2015.

Chun, Wendy Hui Kyong. *Discriminating Data*. Cambridge, MA: MIT Press, 2021.

Clark, T. J. *The Painting of Modern Life: Painting in the Art of Manet and His Followers*. Princeton, NJ: Princeton University Press, 1999.

Cokes, Tony, Carolina Jiménez, Matthew Collin, Frankie Decaiza Hutchinson, Magui Dávila, DeForrest Brown, Jr., et al. *You Got to Get In to Get Out*. Madrid: La Casa Encendida, 2021.

Collin, Matthew. *Altered State: The Story of Ecstasy Culture and Acid House*. London: Serpent's Tail, 2010.

Collin, Matthew. *Rave On: Global Adventures in Electronic Dance Music*. London: Serpent's Tail, 2018.

Colyar, Brock. "New York Nightlife Never Stopped." *New York Magazine*, November 23, 2020. https://www.thecut.com/2020/11/nyc-underground-nightlife-covid-19.html.

Cowley, Patrick. *Mechanical Fantasy Box: The Homoerotic Journal*. San Francisco: Dark Entries Editions, 2019.

Daelyn, J., and Tenika Watson. *My Life Is No Accident*. Middletown, DE: self-published, 2014.

Davis, Heather. *Plastic Matter*. Durham, NC: Duke University Press, 2022.

Dean, Jodi. *Blog Theory: Feedback and Capture in the Circuits of the Drive*. Cambridge: Polity, 2010.

Debord, Guy. *Sick Planet*. Calcutta: Seagull Books, 2008.

Deleuze, Gilles, and Félix Guattari. *What Is Philosophy?* Translated by Hugh Tomlinson and Graham Burchell III. New York: Columbia University Press, 1996.

Denk, Felix, and Sven von Thulen. *Der Klang der Familie: Berlin, Techno, and the Fall of the Wall*. Norderstedt, Germany: BoD, 2014.

Duff, Alvin, and Bambi Lake. *The Unsinkable Bambi Lake*. San Francisco, CA: Manic D, 2017.

Duplan, Anaïs. *Blackspace: On the Poetics of an Afrofuture*. Boston, MA: Black Ocean, 2020.

Dustan, Guillaume. *The Works of Guillaume Dustan*. Vol. 1. Edited by Thomas Clerc. Translated by Daniel Maroun. Los Angeles: Semiotext(e), 2021.

Edelman, Lee. *No Future: Queer Theory and the Death Drive*. Durham, NC: Duke University Press, 2004.

Eichhorn, Kate. *Adjusted Margin: Xerography, Art, and Activism in the Late Twentieth Century*. Cambridge, MA: MIT Press, 2016.

Eshun, Kodwo. *More Brilliant than the Sun*. London: Quartet, 1998.

Eyck, Aldo van. *The Child, the City, and the Artist*. Amsterdam: Sun, 2008.

Fisher, Mark. *K-Punk: The Collected and Unpublished Writings of Mark Fisher*. London: Repeater, 2018.

Fisher, Mark. "The Metaphysics of Crackle." *Dancecult* 5, no. 2 (2013): 42–55.

Fitzpatrick, Cat. *The Call Out*. New York: Seven Stories, 2022.

Fleishmann, T. *Time Is the Thing a Body Moves Through: An Essay*. Minneapolis: Coffeehouse, 2017.

Fournier, Lauren. *Autotheory as Feminist Practice in Art, Writing, and Criticism*. Cambridge, MA: MIT Press, 2021.

Fulton, Nick. "Jasmine Infiniti Makes Deliciously Dark, Apocalyptic Rave Music." *i-D*, April 2, 2020. https://i-d.vice.com/en_uk/article/v74kej /jasmine-infiniti-makes-deliciously-dark-apocalyptic-rave-music.

Gabriel, Kay. *Kissing Other People or the House of Fame*. Sydney: Rosa, 2021.

Galloway, Alexander. *The Interface Effect*. Cambridge: Polity, 2012.

Galloway, Alexander, Eugene Thacker, and McKenzie Wark. *Excommunication: Three Inquires in Media and Mediation*. Chicago: University of Chicago Press, 2013.

Garcia, Luis-Manuel. "An Alternate History of Sexuality in Club Culture." *Resident Advisor*, January 28, 2014. https://ra.co/features/1927.

Geffen, Sasha. *Glitter Up the Dark: How Pop Music Broke the Binary*. Austin: University of Texas Press, 2020.

Genet, Jean. *Our Lady of the Flowers*. New York: Grove, 1994.

Gentili, Cecelia. *Faltas: Letters to Everyone in My Hometown except My Rapist*. New York: Little Puss, 2022.

Georgiakis, Dan, and Marvin Surkin. *Detroit: I Do Mind Dying*. Chicago: Haymarket Books, 2012.

Gilbert, Jeremy. "Psychedelic Socialism." *Open Democracy*, September 22, 2017. https://www.opendemocracy.net/en/psychedelic-socialism/.

Gilbert, Jeremy, and Ewan Pearson. *Discographies: Dance Music, Culture, and the Politics of Sound*. London: Routledge, 1999.

Gilroy, Paul. *Darker than Blue*. Cambridge, MA: Harvard University Press, 2010.

Glück, Robert. *Jack the Modernist*. New York: High Risk, 1985.

Goetsch, Diana. *This Body I Wore*. New York: Farrar, Straus and Giroux, 2022.

Goetz, Rainald. *RAVE*. London: Fitzcarraldo Editions, 2020.

Goldin, Nan. *The Other Side*. Göttingen, Germany: Steidl, 2019.

Goodman, Steve. *Sonic Warfare: Sound, Affect, and the Ecology of Fear*. Cambridge, MA: MIT Press, 2010.

Gornick, Vivian. *The Situation and the Story: The Art of Personal Narrative*. New York: Farrar, Straus and Giroux, 2002.

Gossett, Reina, Eric A. Stanley, and Johanna Burton, eds. *Trap Door: Trans Cultural Production and the Politics of Visibility*. Cambridge, MA: MIT Press, 2017.

Halberstam, Jack. *In a Queer Time and Place*. New York: NYU Press, 2005.

Hall, Stuart. *The Hard Road to Renewal*. London: Verso, 2021.

Hanford, Paul. *Coming to Berlin*. Kent, UK: Velocity, 2022.

Harney, Stefano, and Fred Moten. *The Undercommons: Fugitive Planning and Black Study*. Brooklyn, NY: Minor Compositions, 2013.

Harrison, Harry. *Dreaming in Yellow: The Story of the DiY Sounds System*. Kent, UK: Velocity, 2022.

Heartscape, Porpertine Charity. "Hot Allostatic Load." *New Inquiry*, May 11, 2015. https://thenewinquiry.com/hot-allostatic-load/.

Heartscape, Porpertine Charity. *Psycho Nymph Exile*. London: Arcadia Missa, 2017.

Hebdige, Dick. *Subculture: The Meaning of Style*. London: Routledge, 1979.

Herbert, David. "On the Trail of New York's Nutcracker Kings." *New York Times*, June 13, 2019.

Hocquenghem, Guy. *Homosexual Desire*. Durham, NC: Duke University Press, 1993.

Holman, Jamie, and Alex Zawadzki, eds. *Parties for the People by the People*. London: Rough Trade, 2022.

Hossfeld Etyang, Johannes, Joyce Nyairo, and Florian Sievers, eds. *Ten Cities: Clubbing in Nairobi, Cairo, Kyiv, Johannesburg, Berlin, Naples, Luanda, Lagos, Bristol, Lisbon, 1960–Present*. Leipzig, Germany: Spector Books, 2021.

Hutchinson, Frankie Decaiza. "Club Activism Is Crucial but Will Never Be Enough." In *You Got to Get In to Get Out*, by Tony Cokes et al., 52–63. Madrid: La Casa Encendida, 2021.

Huxtable, Juliana. *Mucus in My Pineal Gland*. New York: Capacious/Wonder, 2017.

Isham, Sultana. "Noise Is the Nigga of Sound." *eflux journal*, no. 117 (April 2021). https://www.e-flux.com/journal/117/387112/noise-is-the-nigga-of-sound/.

Itoh, Takaaki. *Locked Groove Transmission #02*. Accessed May 22, 2022. https://soundcloud.com/lockedgroovebk/locked-groove-transmission-02-takaaki-itoh-part-1-of-2.

Jameson, Fredric. "Future City." *New Left Review*, May/June 2003. https://newleftreview.org/issues/ii21/articles/fredric-jameson-future-city.

Jorn, Asger, and Noël Arnaud. *La Langue Verte*. Paris: Jean-Jacques Pauvet, 1968.

Kleist, Heinrich von. "On the Marionette Theater." Translated by Thomas G. Neumiller. *TDR: The Drama Review* 16, no. 3 (September 1972): 22–26.

Kontra, Gabriella, ed. *Location TBA: Temporary Utopias of Prague Raves*. Prague: Vydalo, 2021.

Koolhaas, Rem. "Junkspace." *October*, no. 100 (Spring 2002): 175–90.

Koolhaas, Rem, et al. *Constant: New Babylon. To Us, Liberty*. Berlin: Hatje Cantze, 2017.

Lady Chablis. *Hiding My Candy: The Autobiography of the Grand Empress of Savanah*. New York: Pocket Books, 1997.

Lawrence, Tim. *Life and Death on the New York Dance Floor, 1980–1983*. Durham, NC: Duke University Press, 2016.

Lawrence, Tim. *Love Saves the Day: A History of American Dance Music Culture, 1970–1979*. Durham, NC: Duke University Press, 2004.

Lipsky, Jessica. "How the Illegal Rave Scene Thrives during the Pandemic." *New York Times*, March 19, 2021. https://www.nytimes.com/2021/03/19/nyregion/illegal-dance-parties-covid-nyc.html.

Lorde, Audre. *Zami: A New Spelling of My Name. A Biomythography*. Berkeley: Crossing, 1982.

Lovink, Geert. *My First Recession: Critical Internet Culture in Transition*. Rotterdam: V2, 2004.

Lovink, Geert. *Social Media Abyss*. Cambridge: Polity, 2016.

Lychee. *Sunrise at Locked Groove 11.13.21*. Accessed May 22, 2022. https://soundcloud.com/lycheefrut/lychee-sunrise-at-locked-groove-11132021.

Mak, Geoffrey. "In Arcadia Ego." *New Models*, October 17, 2019. https://newmodels.io/editorial/issue-1/10-in-arcadia-ego-geoffrey-mak.

Markbreiter, Charlie. "Cruel Poptimism." *New Inquiry*, August 31, 2018. https://thenewinquiry.com/cruel-poptimism/.

Martin, Randy. *Knowledge LTD: Toward a Social Logic of the Derivative*. Philadelphia, PA: Temple University Press, 2015.

McGregor, Fiona. *Buried, Not Dead*. Sydney: Giramondo, 2021.

McGregor, Fiona. *Chemical Palace*. Sydney: Allen & Unwin, 2003.

McKay, George. *Senseless Acts of Beauty: Cultures of Resistance since the Sixties*. London: Verso, 1996.

McQueen, Steve, dir. *Lover's Rock*. London: Turbine Studios, 2020.

Miller, Paul. *Rhythm Science*. Cambridge, MA: MIT Press, 2004.

moore, madison. "DARK ROOM: Sleaze and the Queer Archive." *Contemporary Theater Review* 31, nos. 1–2 (2021): 191–96.

moore, madison. *Fabulous: The Rise of the Beautiful Eccentric*. New Haven, CT: Yale University Press, 2018.

moore, madison. "Hacking into the Now." In *Unter: Rave Posters*, vol. 1, *2015–2020*. Brooklyn, NY: Untermaid Products, 2021.

Moskowitz, P. E. *How to Kill a City*. New York: Nation Books, 2018.

Moss, Jeremiah. *Feral City: On Finding Liberation in Lockdown New York*. New York: Norton, 2022.

Moss, Jeremiah. *Vanishing New York: How a Great City Lost Its Soul*. New York: HarperCollins, 2017.

Moten, Fred. *In the Break: The Aesthetics of the Black Radical Tradition*. Minneapolis: University of Minnesota Press, 2003.

Muggs, Joe. *Bass, Mids, Tops: An Oral History of Sound System Culture*. London: Strange Attractor, 2020.

Muñoz, José Esteban. *Cruising Utopia: The Then and There of Queer Futurity*. New York: NYU Press, 2019.

Nakamura, Lisa. *Digitizing Race*. Minneapolis: University of Minnesota Press, 2007.

Newman, Toni. *I Rise: The Transformation of Toni Newman*. Los Angeles: self-published, 2011.

Newton, Esther. *Mother Camp: Female Impersonators in America*. Chicago: University of Chicago Press, 1979.

Ngai, Sianne. *Our Aesthetic Categories: Zany, Cute, Interesting*. Cambridge, MA: Harvard University Press, 2015.

Nicolai, Olaf, and Jan Wenzel. *Four Times through the Labyrinth*. Leipzig, Germany: Spector Books, 2013.

Niermann, Ingo, and Joshua Simon, eds. *Solution 275–294: Communists Anonymous*. Berlin: Sternberg, 2017.

Nyong'o, Tavia. *Afro-Fabulations*. New York: NYU Press, 2018.

O'Grady, Alice. "Interrupting Flow: Researching Play, Performance and Immersion in Festival Scenes." *Dancecult* 5, no. 1 (May 2013): 18–38.

O'Grady, Alice, and Anna Madill. "Being and Performing 'Older' Woman in Electronic Dance Music Culture." *Dancecult* 11, no. 1 (2019): 7–29.

Ojeda, Iván Monalisa. *Never, Ever Coming Down*. Brooklyn, NY: Sangría, 2016.

Otolith Group. *A Long Time between Suns*. Berlin: Sternberg, 2009.

Pasquinelli, Matteo. *Animal Spirits: A Bestiary of the Common*s. Amsterdam: nai010, 2009.

Peters, Torrey. *Detransition, Baby*. New York: Oneworld, 2021.

Plant, Sadie. *Writing on Drugs*. London: Picador, 2001.

Plant, Sadie. *Zeroes and Ones: Digital Women and the New Technoculture*. London: Fourth Estate, 1997.

Preciado, Paul B. *Counter-sexual Manifesto*. New York: Columbia University Press, 2018.

Preciado, Paul B. *Testo Junkie*. New York: Feminist Press, 2013.

Prestsaeter, Ellef, ed. *These Are Situationist Times!* Oslo: Torpedo, 2020.

Puar, Jasbir. "'I Would Rather Be a Cyborg than a Goddess': Becoming Intersectional in Assemblage Theory." *Transversal* 10 (2012). https://transversal.at/transversal/0811/puar/en.

Raunig, Gerald. *Dividuum*. Los Angeles: Semiotext(e), 2016.

Reynolds, Simon. *Energy Flash: A Journey through Rave Music and Dance Culture*. New York: Soft Skull, 2012.

Reynolds, Simon. *Generation Ecstasy: Into the World of Techno and Rave Culture*. New York: Routledge, 2013.

Rivera, Reynaldo. *Provisional Notes for a Disappeared City*. Los Angeles: Semiotext(e), 2020.

Robinson, Cedric. *Black Marxism: The Making of the Black Radical Tradition*. Chapel Hill: University of North Carolina Press, 2000.

Rodman, Macy. "Berlin." *Neovaginal Dilation Expansion Pack*, vol. 1, *Berlin*. 2020. https://macyrodman.bandcamp.com/album /neovaginal-dilation-expansion-pack-vol-1-berlin.

Rodman, Macy, and Theda Hammel. *Nymphowars*. 2018–20. https:// open.spotify.com/show/1BzoCO242VKeVfd52rupQ6.

Rose, Janus. "Janny's Delivery Service." *Vice*, May 11, 2020. https://www.vice .com/en/article/5dzm7q/why-im-delivering-baked-goods-pandemic.

Rose, Trisha. *Black Noise: Rap Music and Black Culture*. Middletown, CT: Wesleyan, 1994.

Rosenberg, Jordy. Afterword to *Transgender Marxism*, edited by Jules Joanne Gleeson and Elle O'Rourke, 259–95. London: Pluto, 2021.

Rovinelli, Jessica Dunn, dir. *So Pretty*. Brooklyn, NY: 100 Year Films, 2019.

Russell, Legacy. *Glitch Feminism*. Brooklyn, NY: Verso, 2020.

Russom, Gavilán Rayna. "Hostile to Categorization: Initial Elements of a Lineage Study on Techno." In *You Got to Get In to Get Out*, by Tony Cokes et al., 100–119. Madrid: La Casa Encendida, 2021.

Sadler, Simon. *The Situationist City*. Cambridge, MA: MIT Press, 1999.

Salamon, Gayle. *Assuming a Body: Transgender and Rhetorics of Materiality*. New York: Columbia University Press, 2010.

Saldanha, Arun. *Psychedelic White: Goa Trance and Viscosity of Race*. Minneapolis: Minnesota University Press, 2007.

Salkind, Micah. *Do You Remember House? Chicago Queer of Color Undergrounds*. New York: Oxford University Press, 2019.

Schulman, Sarah. *Conflict Is Not Abuse*. Vancouver, Canada: Arsenal Pulp, 2016.

Schulman, Sarah. *The Gentrification of the Mind*. Berkeley: University of California Press, 2013.

Segal. Emily. *Mercury Retrograde*. New York: Deluge Books, 2020.

Serrano, Julia. *Whipping Girl*. New York: Seal, 2016.

Sicko, Dan, *Techno Rebels: The Renegades of Electronic Funk*. Detroit, MI: Wayne State University Press, 2010.

Silcott, Mireille. *Rave America: New School Dancescapes*. Toronto, Canada: ECW Press, 1999.

Snorton, C. Riley. *Black on Both Sides: A Racial History of Trans Identity*. Minneapolis: University of Minnesota Press, 2017.

Solnit, Rebecca, and Joshua Jelly-Schapiro, eds. *Nonstop Metropolis: A New York City Atlas*. Berkeley: University of California Press, 2016.

Spade, Dean. *Mutual Aid: Building Solidarity during This Crisis (and the Next)*. Brooklyn, NY: Verso, 2020.

Stallings, L. H. *Funk the Erotic: Transaesthetics and Black Sexual Cultures*. Urbana: Illinois University Press, 2015.

Stanley, Eric A. *Atmospheres of Violence: Structuring Antagonism and the Trans/Queer Ungovernable*. Durham, NC: Duke University Press, 2021.

St. John, Graham. *Technomad*. London: Equinox, 2009.

Stosuy, Brandon. "On Connecting Your Work to Something Bigger: An Interview with Musician January Hunt." *Creative Independent*, April 27, 2018. https://thecreativeindependent.com/people /january-hunt-on-connecting-your-work-to-something-bigger/.

Strömholm, Christer. *Les Amies de Place Blanche*. Paris: Aman Iman Éditions, 2011.

Stryker, Susan. "Dungeon Intimacies." *parallax* 14, no. 1 (2008): 36–47.

Stryker, Susan. "LA by Night." In *Opposite Sex: Gay Men on Lesbians, Lesbians on Gay Men*, edited by Sara Miles and Eric Rofes, 252–62. New York: New York University Press, 1998.

Sycamore, Mattilda Bernstein. *Freezer Door*. Los Angeles: Semiotext(e), 2020.

Tate, Greg. *Flyboy 2: The Greg Tate Reader*. Durham, NC: Duke University Press, 2016.

Thaemlitz, Terre. *Nuisance: Writings on Identity Jamming and Digital Audio Production*. Vienna: Zanglossus, 2016.

Theweleit, Klaus. *Male Fantasies*. Vol. 1, *Women, Floods, Bodies, Histories*. Minneapolis: University of Minnesota Press, 1987.

Thom, Kai Cheng. *I Hope We Choose Love*. Vancouver, Canada: Arsenal Pulp, 2019.

Thornton, Sarah. *Club Cultures: Music, Media, and Subcultural Capital*. Middletown, CT: Wesleyan University Press, 1996.

thunderfunk, cranberry. *outer][space*. Brooklyn, NY: self-published, 2021.

Treichler, Paula. *How to Have a Theory in an Epidemic*. Durham, NC: Duke University Press, 1999.

Trieu, Kato. *Future Subject Matter*. New York: Exmiliary, 2021.

Tucker, Ricky. *And the Category Is . . .* Boston: Beacon, 2021.

Underground Resistance. *Interstellar Fugitives*. Detroit: Underground Resistance, 1988.

Vadim, Roger, dir. *Barbarella*. Paris: Marianne Productions, 1968.

van der Elsken, Ed. *Love on the Left Bank*. London: André Deutsch, 1956.

van der Heide, Bart, ed. *Techno/Globalization/Pandemic*. Stuttgart: Hatje Cantz, 2021.

van Veen, Tobias C. "Technics, Precarity and Exodus in Rave Culture." *Dancecult* 1, no. 2 (2010): 29–47.

Vitos, Botond. "Along the Lines of the Roland TB-303: Three Perversions of Acid Techno." *Dancecult* 6, no. 1 (2014): 2014. https://dj.dancecult.net/index.php/dancecult/article/view/460.

von Reinhold, Shola. *LOTE*. London: Jacaranda Books, 2020.

Walker, Harron. "Mounting." Substack newsletter, no. 6 (March 30, 2020).

Wallenhorst, Maxi. "Like a Real Veil, Like a Bad Analogy: Dissociative Style and Trans Aesthetics." *eflux journal*, no. 117 (April 2021). https://www.e-flux.com/journal/117/385637/like-a-real-veil-like-a-bad-analogy-dissociative-style-and-trans-aesthetics/.

Wark, McKenzie. *Reverse Cowgirl*. Los Angeles: Semiotext(e), 2020.

Weheliye, Alexander. *Phonographies: Grooves in Sonic Afro-Modernity*. Durham, NC: Duke University Press, 2005.

Williams, Terry. *Soft City: Sex for Business and Pleasure in New York City.* New York: Columbia University Press, 2022.

Witt, Emily. "Clubbing Is a Lifeline—and It's Back." *New Yorker*, June 24, 2021. https://www.newyorker.com/culture/dept-of-returns/clubbing -is-a-lifeline-and-its-back.

Zaveri, Mihir. "Rave under the Kosciuszko Bridge." *New York Times*, August 8, 2020. https://www.nytimes.com/2020/08/08/nyregion/nyc -illegal-parties.html.